In *A Promised Life*, Robert Maxwell, Missionary to the Punjab, 1900-1941, Elizabeth Paige Maxwell McRight skillfully weaves together her grandfather's story through rich descriptive narrative and passages from his letters and those of other family members. McRight's account takes on a life of its own, with concrete descriptions of place, time, home life in the United States and the contrasting cultural reality of India.

A Promised Life is a worthy addition to American and global history covering two world wars. Yet the book does not let us forget the living, breathing, human stories which are embodied in concept of "his-story."

Nancy Owen Nelson, PhD
author of *Searching for Nannie B: Connecting Three Generations of Southern Women* (memoir);
author of *My Heart Wears No Colors* (poetry, pub. 11/18)

A PROMISED LIFE

Robert Maxwell: Missionary to the Punjab 1900-1942

ELIZABETH PAIGE MAXWELL MCRIGHT

WestBow
PRESS®
A DIVISION OF THOMAS NELSON
& ZONDERVAN

Copyright © 2018 Elizabeth Paige Maxwell McRight.

All rights reserved. No part of this book may be used or reproduced by any means, graphic, electronic, or mechanical, including photocopying, recording, taping or by any information storage retrieval system without the written permission of the author except in the case of brief quotations embodied in critical articles and reviews.

This book is a work of non-fiction. Unless otherwise noted, the author and the publisher make no explicit guarantees as to the accuracy of the information contained in this book and in some cases, names of people and places have been altered to protect their privacy.

Scripture taken from the King James Version of the Bible.

WestBow Press books may be ordered through booksellers or by contacting:

WestBow Press
A Division of Thomas Nelson & Zondervan
1663 Liberty Drive
Bloomington, IN 47403
www.westbowpress.com
1 (866) 928-1240

Because of the dynamic nature of the Internet, any web addresses or links contained in this book may have changed since publication and may no longer be valid. The views expressed in this work are solely those of the author and do not necessarily reflect the views of the publisher, and the publisher hereby disclaims any responsibility for them.

Any people depicted in stock imagery provided by Getty Images are models, and such images are being used for illustrative purposes only. Certain stock imagery © Getty Images.

ISBN: 978-1-9736-3252-8 (sc)
ISBN: 978-1-9736-3254-2 (hc)
ISBN: 978-1-9736-3253-5 (e)

Library of Congress Control Number: 2018907682

Print information available on the last page.

WestBow Press rev. date: 09/07/2018

For Bill and Robert McRight,
so they can know more about the men for whom they
are named and the times in which they lived.

PREFACE

The journey to discover the story of my grandfather's life reminded me that we tend to see family members through the lens of loving relationship, larger than life in importance, and yet we are often too close (or too far removed) to see the impact of those lives on the larger world. When I began, I knew that my grandfather, Robert Maxwell, who died when I was three days old, was a careful biblical scholar who translated a chapter from the Hebrew and a chapter from the Greek every morning before breakfast. I knew that he was a strict disciplinarian and a man who loved his sons and wanted the best for them, regardless of what they personally desired. What I knew about his father was that he was a man who kept his promise; he survived a Confederate prison camp and lived into his nineties, having raised a farmer's family and educated one son for the ministry, as he had pledged to do while praying to survive that prison.

These taciturn New Englanders were self-effacing people who would not have wanted attention paid to them. They felt a sense of duty to raise sons and daughters who would make their own contributions to their communities. Their story is part of the larger tale of the spread of the gospel far beyond their own households. They are not particularly remarkable on the world stage, yet their story points beyond themselves to represent the countless others who devoted their lives to being Christ's witnesses.

In 2010, I spent Thanksgiving weekend with my cousin, Anne Maxwell, in Philadelphia. She showed me letters our great-aunt, Elizabeth Maxwell, saved, letters my grandfather had written home to his family from the mission field. Anne wondered what we should do with the letters. Since our grandfather had been a missionary in what is now Pakistan for forty-two years, I was pretty sure that the

vii

thing to do was give the letters to the Presbyterian Historical Society, near my cousin's home in Philadelphia. I was sure that those family letters would have historical value for people who study life in the mission field during the late nineteenth and early twentieth centuries.

Anne retrieved the letters from a closet; they were in an old cardboard box. It smelled dusty and was packed full of thin letters written on onionskin paper. We tried to read a few of the handwritten letters, but then to our relief, Grandfather somehow got access to a typewriter.

Thus began a journey to discover more about my grandfather's life story. When I was in college and home for summers, I would get my dad to tell me stories about his childhood in India and about life back in the States after he came back at age twelve. The year my father died, I wrote a set of those stories down for my brother and his children for Christmas.

Years later, I took a trip to upstate New York with Anne's parents and my husband, and I got to learn more about my grandparents. We stopped at the farmhouse where my grandfather grew up. I met Mary, Uncle Charlie's daughter, who was just a little thing when my own father lived with them. She remembered Daddy's blue eyes. It was that day I learned about George Small Maxwell's vow when he was a prisoner of the Confederacy: if the Lord let him live, he would raise one of his sons to enter the ministry.

A search for my grandfather's father's Civil War records did not uncover any documents but did introduce me to a cousin, Marion Redding, related through the Maxwell family. She enjoys genealogy and was glad to have the facts I know and a copy of the genealogy that my grandmother, Maud, had requested when she was applying for membership in the DAR. This cousin had posted family pictures, including one of George I had never seen and Elizabeth's wedding picture when, at the age of sixty-two, she became the third wife of her first cousin, Robert J. Maxwell.

That fall, I finally took the letters to Philadelphia and gave them to the Historical Society. I also spent a week in Atlanta, where I met Dr. Raj Nadella, a professor at Columbia Theological Seminary who was born in India. Though his field is New Testament, he is very interested in the great missionary movement through which so many in his homeland became Christian. The following spring, I happened to see Dr. Nadella again at Columbia Seminary. He had read some of my family's letters and told me that they pointed to a time when missionaries helped to change the culture of India. By their acceptance of the untouchables and other lower classes and by their education of girls as well as boys, the missionaries helped the masses of people in India. They showed them the possibilities of a future for themselves different from the limits of the lives their families had known for generations. Grandfather's letters from the early years showed few converts to Christianity among the students and their families, but the seeds were being sown for a new life for India and for the independent states of Bangladesh and Pakistan.

When I visited my cousin, Anne, in the spring of 2013, I stopped by the Historical Society to check a few things in the minutes of the General Assembly of the United Presbyterian Church in North America. On that visit, the reference librarian helped me to find four folders of correspondence between Grandfather and the foreign mission board secretary, his good friend from the mission field, Dr. W. B. Anderson. These letters cover the years following the end of Aunt Elizabeth's letters. They picture a missionary who, having struggled for four years to pass his language exams when he first went to India, later became the chief translator and secretary of his mission area. They tell of a preacher and teacher who became an administrator involved in school and hospital administration, a respected leader closely involved in planning for expansion of the mission and called upon to work for reconciliation and discipline when there was difficulty between people or abuse of church office.

Reading Grandfather's letters was a good reminder that no matter our hopes and intentions, we cannot presume to change a culture or impose on its people our own assumptions about the way the world works. The missionaries did bring education and health care to what is now Pakistan, but the people they found were from a tribal culture of many faiths and loyalties. In writing this book, I have drawn heavily on his letters as well as on the records of his college and seminary years, on my memories of the stories I heard as a young woman, and on my own experience of the places in this country where my grandfather lived and studied. Because we are a family who loves

ix

story, I have several times put events in terms of story rather than just recount the basic facts of the situation. In every case, I have tried to be faithful to the stories as I received them.

In 1947, five years after my grandparents came home, what had been the British colony of India became the independent nations of India and Pakistan. The Christian faith is one among many religions in Pakistan and one for which people still die in some areas. Robert Maxwell recognized the limits of his own vision. When he was discouraged, he wrote to his friend the foreign mission secretary that we cannot know what the outcome will be, but in everything, we can rely on the loving-kindness of our God. Such humble trust is a good example to all of us who share his heritage of faith.

CHAPTER

1

George Small Maxwell's Vow: 1864–1890

The call came for chow time, and here came the mess hands ladling out a meager cup of thin gruel. No bread today. No rats caught last night, either. They had either found a night of rest and mating more to their liking that spring night than foraging, or all had finally been caught and roasted on campfires. Rumor was that the Union was winning, thanks be to God. They had cut the supply lines to the Rebels at Atlanta, and word was that Sherman was marching to Savannah and the sea, burning fields in his path. Maybe the war would end, but in the meantime, would prisoners of this Confederate Army survive? If the rebels didn't have enough to feed their army and their kin, they would not have to spare for their captives. Since Vicksburg, when defeated prisoners had gone on to fight in Chattanooga after being released to go home, there had been no more prisoner exchanges. Andersonville was called a prison, but in truth, it was just a small stockade, about sixteen acres, George judged, surrounded by log fence fifteen feet high.

George sank down on a rock to drink his dinner. When it was gone, he circled his thigh with his thumb and middle finger. How long would he last? In a month, if he lived, he would be thirty-three. Remembering Margaret and the children (George, Mary, and

William), he thought of John Telford, Margaret's brother, who had written before he left and went to war. John was a devout preacher and man of deep faith. When George left for the fight, John had prayed for him and written counseling him to remember that God has something to do with everything that takes place and will be glorified and bring good to his people out of the worst of things. Looking up to heaven, George prayed to God, vowing that if he would deliver him from the prison alive and restore him to his family, he would educate a son for God's ministry.

George was raised on Scotch Hill on a family farm that had been claimed by four Maxwell brothers shortly after the Revolution. He had known Margaret Telford all her life. Her family farm was near his. Their families worshipped together in the United Presbyterian Church in North America (UPNA) congregation in East Greenwich, and they had spent their young days socializing with the UPNA young people in Cambridge, Greenwich, and Salem, the three closest churches in their presbytery. George wanted more for his family than they could have on Scotch Hill. The farm was too small for all the Maxwells crowded in there. Margaret had family in western Pennsylvania, and they knew people even farther west through the church, so they and some neighbors headed west to Iowa to farm.

He had had some good seasons working land on shares, but then the war came, and he joined up. It was the right thing to do to stop the South's secession from the Union and to end the slave trade. Farms in New York and Iowa made it fine without slaves. The Southern farms could do it, too. It was true that slavery was an institution described in scripture, but what he had heard about the conditions in which Southern slaves were kept surely was not what Paul meant when he said in Ephesians 6:9, "Masters, do not threaten your slaves for you know that both of you have the same Master in heaven who shows no partiality." Living in a tent through the winter in Andersonville, George knew if he lived, he would join Margaret and the children at home in New York and do what he could to help his father and brothers' farm, at least until he got his strength back.

AUGUST 14, 1871

The cry of a baby, strong and lusty, suddenly replaced Margaret's labor cries. George had come in to meet this new child after Mary ran to the hayfield to tell him that Aunt Agnes had sent her to say that the baby was coming. Now as Agnes opened the bedroom door, Margret smiled and said, "Come and see what the Lord has provided in answer to your vow. The boy is here who will keep your promise." A son for the ministry. He would be Robert, like many Maxwell men before him, and take his place among the ministers in the Telford and Cree families on his mother's side. George had thought that the child born first when he came back to Scotch Hill after the war might be the son he had promised, but little Elizabeth, now four, had been that child. Her sister Mary had been thrilled to have another girl in the family. Three years later, he had looked for a son when Anna Belle arrived. The girls would be a help to Margaret once Mary, now already thirteen, was grown and married off. St. Paul was right that the Lord is able to do far more than ever we can ask or think.

George cradled his son in his arms as he offered a prayer of thanksgiving for this gift and renewed his promise before he gave Robert back to his mother; he thanked Agnes for her help and went back to see how young George and William were coming with the hay. They would be glad for the news. The baby's birth meant that they were now free to be farmers like they wanted. At fifteen, George was done with schooling, and William, at eleven, would rather be in the fields than in the books. He had loved this farm and being among his cousins and grandparents since the moment they returned. George knew either boy would have gone on to school if he made him, but it would have been against the nature God had given them. Young Robert would never know a day that he was not destined for the ministry. He would learn farming as he grew; the farm used all the hands it had in season, but he would be expected to study, to finish high school and go on to college and seminary, too, to prepare for his calling. George and Margaret would see to that. Margaret had said it today, and she had said many times how she hoped to raise a son for the ministry, like her grandfather, John Cree, and her brothers, John Cree and Morrison Samuel Telford, her twin. Well, Margaret had her prayer answered too. And God would preserve this boy given to fulfill his father's promise. George was sure of that.

***

Following Robert's birth, two more sons were born to George and Margaret: David in 1873 and Charles in 1875. By 1890, the two oldest children were married. Mary married John Alexander in 1879; by 1890, their family included Flora and Frank. George had waited until he could buy his own farm and make a start. He married Anna Mary Arnott in 1885, and they had added Marion and Beth to their family. The life of the farm went on steadily.

After George left, William was his father's right hand in the fields, and Robert worked hard as well, laying by all he could earn as a farmer's helper for his tuition. Elizabeth and Anna Belle were useful aids to their mother with the garden and household chores, able to step in and cover for others as needed when there was illness. Both of them were glad for the times when they could play with their little nieces and nephew on Sunday afternoons when the family gathered after church. In due time, Anna Belle would have her own family, but the years when the household was just beginning to expand to the next generation, the years before Robert would leave them for school and for good, were happy days as the younger girls grew into their own place in the church and family.

With hay for their own cattle and horses (plus some to sell in good years), corn and oats for the family and the livestock, potatoes for a cash crop, the kitchen garden and the apple trees, there was always something growing that needed tending, from last frost in late May until the first hard freeze in late September or early October, when the potatoes had to be out of the ground. The livestock needed tending all year long, of course, and well repaid their board in butter, milk, eggs, and meat. In winter, the permafrost was up to four feet deep, so nothing grew. The girls learned to can the fresh vegetables that could not overwinter in the cold cellar, where root vegetables and apples were stored.

In winter, train cars packed full of huge blocks of ice from Lake George headed south, where the ice would be sold to people with

A PROMISED LIFE

iceboxes. It was not easy to imagine places so warm even in winter that people would need such things, but George's stories of the South in wartime made it believable. He had lived outside in a tent in winter. Here, where the temperature in January often dipped into single digits and below at night and the snow covered the top wire of the fences, it would not be possible to live long outside. Winter was time for mending tack and tools, sewing and knitting, and writing long letters to family members and church friends who now lived far from home. It was time for learning all one could of the faith through daily study of scripture and the catechism and learning of the ways of the world as often as the news could be delivered.

***

The world outside the farm was changing, with European powers claiming other lands as colonies and protectorates. America was growing, with Wyoming slated to become the forty-fourth state in 1890, the first state in which women would have the vote. It seemed those suffragettes had finally gotten what they had been campaigning for, in at least one state. Robert would be a missionary in a strange new world. Who knew where he would go or what the place would be like when he got there? Thanks be to God that he had been spared in this fever, even though he was still slowly recovering. Life was secure in the family, but it was not without its own seasons of pain and loss.

Elizabeth brought in the mail and opened a letter from Washington Academy. She had sent word to the school of David's death, and now she read the reply:

Salem, New York March 13, 1890

My dear Miss Maxwell,
    I enclose a set of resolutions which were prepared by the pupils of our department in regard to the loss of our dear friend David.
    Believe me we are all most sincere in our sympathy for you all. I received your letter last

5

night. How great a comfort to be able to say with full assurance "it is well with the child."

Affectionately yours,
Sara L. Gardiner[1]

At the morning session of the Academic Department of Washington Academy, Monday March 10, 1890 a committee consisting of Miss Cora Irwin and Mr.'s Taft and Gibson were appointed to prepare resolutions upon the death of David S. Maxwell. The following were submitted and accepted as the expressions of the teachers and pupils of Washington Academy

Whereas It has pleased the All-wise Father to take to himself our friend and school mate, David S. Maxwell, therefore be it –

Resolved: that by his removal we have lost a true and faithful friend, and the school an earnest, cheerful worker.

Resolved: that at appreciating those qualities of honor, truth and faithfulness which so endeared him to his teachers and school mates we will strive to emulate them and act well our part in life.

Resolved: that we extend our earnest, heartfelt sympathy to the family of our friend in this their hour of bereavement and sorrow.

Resolved: that a copy of these resolutions be sent to his parents, and that they be printed in the village papers.

Jas. Gibson, Jr., T.J. Taft, Cora Irwin.

It was a fitting tribute, Elizabeth thought, and would be a comfort to Mother and Father. Such a sad time. The household had been shut up with sick folks for days; Robert, Davey, and Charlie were all down with scarlet fever. The others seemed to be getting better now, but it had been too much for Davey. There had been so much of death and sickness in the family. Mother's older sisters, Aunt Agnes and Aunt Mary Jane, had died within months of each other in '87, and now Frank Alexander, Mary's boy, was gone February 25 and Davey, two weeks later. To lose a nephew and a brother so close was almost too much grief to bear, but Elizabeth knew that theirs was not the only family to lose folks, and their grief would be shared by others.

Uncle John had said, "You are the best correspondent I ever had among my relations."

It was a thing that she could do, even though she sometimes spent weeks at a time in bed with illness herself. By twenty, she had become the family correspondent, and so she had written to the family and to the school the day Davey died.

She opened Matie's letter next:

East Greenwich, New York March 11, 1890

Dear Libbie and all,

I would like so much to see you all but as I cannot, I will write you a few lines. We did not hear of Davie's sickness until we heard of his death. I cannot tell you how much I feel for and sympathize with you. May God help you to bear this sore trial. May Jesus be to you a friend that sticketh closer than a brother. There is a verse I think in Ecclesiastes but I'm not sure which has often comforted me. It is this: though a sinner do evil 100 times and his days be prolonged, yet surely, I know that it shall be well with them that fear God, which fear before him.

I am sorry to hear Libbie that you do not gain any faster, hope you will soon be better.

There seems to be a great deal of sickness. How thankful anyone ought to be who is well. I had a letter from Uncle John last week. He said there were a great many sick where they are. The roads were so bad he visited them on horseback.

George, I thought you would like to read my paper. I will send it to you. I would have given it to him Sabbath night but one-page I had changes after writing it, and I wanted to fix it a bit. I hope you will not mind the mistakes. I do not think it is put together in very good shape. You need not bother to send it back. I wrote it on brown paper first.

Belle, we miss you ever so much at the young people's meeting.

Love to all.
Matie

Please excuse my mistakes. I have too many same.

It would be good to see Matie and the others, but Elizabeth knew that was a selfish wish. She could not want them exposed to the illness that had taken her brother and her nephew.

The last letter was from Maud Haney in New Wilmington, Pennsylvania:

New Wilmington
March 11, 1890

My dear Libbie,

I just heard yesterday through Mrs. Houston, of the sickness in your family, and of the death of Davey. It seems so sad. He seemed the least likely to be taken. I always thought of him as being so healthy and full of life. I hope the rest are better, and hope your sister, Mrs. Alexander, won't get down. When she said she was taking care of you, she said her little boy died also. I don't remember ever seeing him, but it will be a hard stroke on his mother. Lizzie was here yesterday, the first time I've seen her to talk to long since she came home. We went to visit the Philo

A PROMISED LIFE

society in the evening; Miss Telford had a critical essay. I heard that Rob expected to come here next year. Is that so? It would seem like home to see him here.

I had the grip, but not as bad as you. I guess I was in bed eight days and not strong yet. It's terribly weakening. Well Libbie, write as soon as you are able to do so, without injury to yourself. Hoping to hear of your recovery, also all the family.

With much sympathy and love,
Maud Haney

PS Mother wishes to send you her love and hope that will all soon be well. Maud

Maud had heard right about Robert. He would go off to New Wilmington to start college in the fall. Had he been able to start last fall, he might have missed the fever, but he had been at home and so would spend the rest of spring regaining his strength, God willing, and helping with the planting before he went off to school. The grip was bad. While the boys were ill with the fever, Elizabeth and Belle were down with grip and of no use to Mother. That's why poor Mary had to be at their house, even as she mourned her own loss, but it had seemed that taking care of her brothers and sisters helped to ease her pain. At least, Elizabeth hoped so, just as she hoped these letters would be of help to Mother and to Father.

There was also a letter from Rev. H. S. MacAyeal that was for Elizabeth particularly. The MacAyeals had been with the church for many years but now were off in Nebraska because the weather there was better for his asthma. Rev. MacAyeal thoughtfully included an outline of a sermon on Hebrews 4:3: "we who have believed enter that rest." It was such a help to have words of comfort from her old pastor. Elizabeth loved his sermons, and this one reflecting on Davey's death was a special treasure. Just as important were his words of encouragement to her:

I am so glad to know that things go on so well at home. One soweth & another reapeth but the harvest is the Lord's. I hope to see much fruit from the field there. I was so sorry to know if you're being sick & I'm equally happy to hear of you getting around again. May the Lord long spare you to the home & the church. You may think you are not of much use as an invalid, but sometimes God blesses the whole community & church for the life & prayers of a single individual.[2]

Many days, Elizabeth (sometimes called Libby) felt completely useless as she lay in bed, too weak to help her mother with the cooking and cleaning or out in the garden. To think that she could be a blessing to the community and her church with her prayers, even in her weakness, was comfort indeed.

Aunt Annie wrote. It seemed a special comfort to Mother to hear from her twin brother's wife:

To Mrs. Margaret Maxwell
March 15, 1890
Study of MS Telford
Pastor of the UPA church
Wurttemberg, Pennsylvania

Dear sister and family:

We received your good letter yesterday. We were so anxious to know how you all are and to have a fuller account of David's illness and death. What can I say to comfort you in this hour of trial? I am sure I can sympathize with you as few can, for my girlhood days were shrouded in a dark cloud by this same dread disease. Two brothers, with whom I had played for years, were taken away after 36 hours sickness. Father never recovered from the loss of those boys. When he was nearing his close of life, he spoke of them as he had often done that the hope of his life had gone out when they were taken away.

It is a dread disease for so many reasons. All ages are liable to it, and in itself it is a terror, not to speak of the dregs it often leaves as a heritage of weakness, to those who have had it. When those who have it are sent away from all others, it makes it very lonely. Our older children had it, and I would not be much afraid of their taking it again, but Bertie has never had it. Winnie was never very strong after he had scarlet fever; he had throat trouble and was nervous I think to a greater degree than he would have been. I do hope Libby will be spared an attack of it.

God's ways are truly past finding out. Cannot see why the young man of promise should be called away just as he began to show signs of usefulness and to be able to speak for the Master, while so many take no thought for these things. "Even so Father, for so it seemeth good in Thy sight." It is God's way, and we carry out the same principle when we would seek for fruit, we take the ripest and the choicest, allowing that which is not matured to remain; by the sunshine and shower it may become fit for use. If we have one in our household that gives evidence of a well-ordered life, of a closer walk with the Master then another, we should rejoice that that one is taken, and yet it is not easy to give up our jewels. Oh for faith to say, fully meaning what we say, "He doeth all things well." "What I do thou knowest not now but thou shalt know hereafter."

What a blessed promise; the Bible is so full of them, and yet we go sorrowing as if left without anything to comfort in our many trials and bereavements that befall us on our journey from earth to heaven. Robbie and Charlie should be very careful for a long while; the healing time is very dangerous. So liable to cold and no one can afford to risk the sequels to this fearful disease. I had it in a comparatively mild form when my brothers died but was never so sick with anything else.

Have a letter from Maggie last eve; she is well and kept very busy. We will send her your latest letter. We hope to hear from some of the friends often. So glad Sarah is able to be with you. It is good to have company in such trial. We look for Winnie home this evening.

Must close and write to Maggie. I always write Saturday evening to mail on Monday. She is very conscientious about mailing anything in the latter part of the week to have it passing through the mails on Sabbath. We are having a regular March snow alternating shower today, rain and sunshine and snow alternating.

Much love from all to all. I would have posted sooner but had company all week and Mrs. T can get away easier to write than I can.

Your loving sister Annie

PS have you a picture of David? I do not remember any of your children younger than Libby never saw any of the boys. I think I saw Anna but am not sure. Think we surely will visit you before long. Our aunt Kate talks of coming back and then I can get away better. Hoping to have it good tidings from you, I am yours lovingly, Annie[3]

Davey had been full of promise, so devout and so well thought of. He could have been a second fulfillment to Father's promise, but that was not to be. God does all things well, but sometimes God's ways, which are not our ways, are beyond understanding.

CHAPTER
2

Years of Study: 1892–1899

COLLEGE OF NEW JERSEY

Robert stepped out of his boarding house and inhaled the rich morning air filled, as it always was when the wind blew just right, with the aroma of cow barn. The farm which supplied much of the town's dairy products, rich milk and creamy fresh butter, was three miles from campus but the smell of cow in the morning carries far. Robert thought of home and Charlie up milking before daylight. It was one of the things he did not miss about home.

Princeton had been the right move. Freshman year at Westminster, several of the faculty to whom he confided his call to mission service encouraged him to get to know the world beyond the Presbyterian Church in North America in his college years. He would be back among the flock in seminary at Allegheny soon enough, but these years in Princeton would be a chance to mingle with people of different backgrounds, people who saw the world from different perspectives. The sons of New York bankers and New Jersey politicians and businessmen were not the boys he knew from home. Many had gone to prep school together from early days. Robert smiled to himself as he recalled his own school days. He had studied and received good marks, but he could never have been ready for Princeton right out of

Washington Academy. The year at Westminster had given him a good chance to develop study skills for higher learning. He had to apply himself, but it had all been for the best. Now he was studying with some of the best prepared undergraduates, and while he would never distinguish himself, he could keep his head above water in classes. He was grateful to God for a good mind to apply to his studies. So much of the joy of life depended on one's perspective.

Some of his classmates described hot and cold running water in the tubs at home and daily baths, if they wanted one. Some of those same classmates complained bitterly that they had to bathe in the gym and only on Wednesdays and Saturdays, when showers were available to students. Twice a week showering or bathing in clean water you did not have to draw from the well for Mother to heat on the stove so you could share it with your brothers in a tin tub that you got to use first only every third week was really pretty grand when it came to it. He could not feel too smug about those other men, though. With the crash of the stock market earlier in the year, banks closing, businesses failing, unemployment at 25 percent in Pennsylvania and 35 percent in New York, according to the papers, many of his classmates worried about their families back home and their own chances of completing their education. He knew this from random comments they dropped, even if they brushed them off with manly bravado as soon as the words were said.

There was more pride here and more hazing than he had known at Westminster. Still, the prevailing mood was of a democratic spirit, that we are all of us College of New Jersey men together. He had been warmly welcomed to the class ranks of the class of '96 when he arrived and quickly initiated into the fall rituals of football and other forms of rivalry with Yale that made college life exciting. He had not joined an eating club. Those were the places where the social cliques seemed to be fully formed, exclusive places that bred a snobbishness he despised. It seemed the opposite of the Christian charity we are called to share with all. Still there were many who shared his view and shunned the eating clubs for simple fare in other places, places like the boarding house, where he took most of his meals.

He was preparing for service in a world of chaos, Robert realized, yet it was still our Father's world, and in his provident plan, all would be well. The news in the papers, free in the school's library, told of much unrest, not only in North America but abroad as well. British soldiers attacked by six thousand native warriors in Africa. Hawaiian resistance to white professionals and businessmen had led to the overthrow of the queen. And the social order was being shaken at home and abroad, as well. New Zealand this year gave women the vote in national elections, unheard of in the rest of the world, but Colorado allowed women to vote in state elections, joining Wyoming and Utah. The world was changing, and Robert was determined to be ready for what God would have him do in this new world.

This fall term, he was taking two hours of Latin, four of Greek, three of math, two of history, two of biology, one of Bible, and two of French. The Latin he had had in high school. The Greek he would use as a pastor. It was not exactly the Greek of the New Testament, but the language was not so different that it would not help, and reading the classics in Greek would be fascinating when he got good at it. History had turned out to be the best. Dr. Woodrow Wilson was a teacher who could make history live for you. He asked wonderful questions about world events, ancient and modern, and really made a man think. He was also the coach for debate, and that was a real stroke of good fortune.

Realizing that a missionary had need to be well spoken and able to answer quickly with counter-arguments, Robert had immediately joined Whig, one of the two debate societies on campus, housed in small almost identical Greek marble buildings, side by side, in the center of campus. Both societies had been founded in the 1760s and had honed the debate skills of the likes of James Madison and Aaron Burr when they were students at Princeton, Robert had learned when he first entered the hallowed hall of Whig. Debates were lively, and voices rang out in the evening air as members practiced for debates between Whig and Clio, the other house, and for the rarer debates with students from other colleges. Whig held her own, and Robert was beginning to see his way to do his part. Dr. Wilson's gentle coaching helped. Watching the skill with which upperclassmen argued their points helped at least as much as Robert formed his argument for his own attempts at debate.

***

Robert seemed to be happy at Princeton, Elizabeth thought as she read his letter. She had wondered why he wanted to leave their own denomination's school in New Wilmington, but as she heard him explain his logic to Father, it had made sense. Even in Cambridge, disagreements among Presbyterians had led to church splits back even to Great-Grandfather John Maxwell's day as an elder in the Coila church. At one time, there had been four Presbyterian churches in Cambridge. If Robert was to cooperate with people from various denominations and backgrounds on the mission field and to approach the Hindus and Muslims with a winsome presentation of the gospel, he was right to want to spend his college years among people with different ideas and backgrounds.

Father and Charlie missed Robert sorely this second harvest season without him. With Davey gone in '90, it meant hard labor for them. George and William and cousin R. J. pitched in all they could, but they had their own farms to see to. Mother kept everyone fed and in clean and mended clothes, and Elizabeth and Belle tended the chickens and the kitchen garden all the time. Now that the apples were in, there would be apple butter for the bread and canned apples for pies this winter. It was good to be able to make her own contributions to the family larder. Setting aside Robert's letter til she could share it with the family at supper, Elizabeth prayed that God would keep him strong and well this year and bless his studies as he prepared for his calling to serve in the Lord's ministry. Charlie was just mean sometimes, saying that Robert had an easy life there in school in New Jersey, while he had to shoulder the load at home. Robert didn't seek the ministry. He was the one Father had promised for it, and Elizabeth was sure that life in Princeton with all those courses, even three languages, was no easy berth. She prayed earnestly for God to watch over her little brother.

***

The years seemed to fly by. In his senior year, Robert had to decide about seminary. He had prayed earnestly about the decision. Fred Loetcher, a PCUSA Presbyterian and fellow member of Whig, had talked to Robert about joining him at Princeton Seminary. It was a fine school in many ways, with leading scholars, Robert knew, but like the college, it had its eating clubs, dens of iniquity, and producers of cliques and divisions. It made no sense in a seminary, and at any rate, for all its renown, the school was really too liberal in its theology. It was closer to home, and he would have fifteen friends from college there, but Robert had applied to Allegheny, his own UPNA seminary near Pittsburgh; word came in early March that he was accepted. Today, he would be part of the last graduating class of the College of New Jersey. When the fall term began, the school would henceforth be known as Princeton University. He would graduate with the college's first class of Phi Beta Kappa graduates, and while he did not qualify for membership himself, he was glad to see that his alma mater was joining the prestigious ranks of those schools that honored academic excellence in students and was glad for his friends who were members of this first class of the chapter in Princeton.

When Robert woke on graduation day, he prayed for his classmates who would scatter to take up lives of meaning and service of various kinds (he hoped in every case), and he prayed especially for all who like himself would be entering seminary in the fall to continue preparing to serve as pastors and teachers in Christ's church. Finally, he prayed for his family at home, busy with planting now that the weather was fair and, if it were God's will, that he might know the joy of family life when his years of preparation were finished.

***

ALLEGHENY SEMINARY

The stated clerk of Argyle Presbytery wrote to the president of Allegheny Seminary to attest that Robert Maxwell was a candidate in good standing. It was a seminary admission requirement. It seemed that everyone the Maxwells knew had always known what Robert's life work would be. Seminary began the first Wednesday in October each year. The clerk of session also wrote to inform the seminary that Robert was a member of the church, baptized as an infant, and an active member from the age of fourteen; that his piety and deportment were above reproach; and that the session had recommended him to the presbytery as a suitable candidate for ministry before he was received and had never had reason to consider withdrawing that recommendation. The transcript of his work at the College of New Jersey had been sent.

Everything seemed to be in order, so before Robert dressed to go milk, he knelt to pray that as he shared the letter informing him that he was accepted into the fall's entering class, his family would rejoice with him. Later, when he came to the house for lunch, Elizabeth greeted him with the news that she had put his letter from the seminary at his place at the table. So it happened that in the presence of his family, after Father returned thanks for the meal and the hands that had prepared it and prayed God's blessing on the food and on the labors of the family, Robert shared his letter and the news that soon he would be packing a bag and boxing up his books for a move to the seminary in Allegheny, Pennsylvania, just outside Pittsburgh.

No one seemed at all surprised. It was God's will that he should be a minister. God had provided the way. Father offered a second prayer of thanksgiving for the news and prayed that God would bless Robert's studies in the seminary. When Robert opened his eyes after everyone joined in the "Amen," Mother was smiling softly with what seemed to be tears in her eyes. Again, Robert was reminded that this calling was a promise shared by all his family.

As Robert left the house to get back to the day's work, taking down a dead tree and reducing it to stove wood, Elizabeth stood by the door. She walked a way with him and gave her own promise that she would be faithful in prayer and in correspondence during his years of seminary and that she would send fresh cookies to sweeten his studies from time to time.

Next Lord's day, following the presbytery meeting after worship, Robert's pastor let him know that the presbytery had authorized the seminary to grant him the princely sum of $125 for the year ahead. Robert thanked him and then quietly thanked God for the providential support he felt from family and church alike, as he walked in faith the next part of the path laid out for him.

***

When he traveled to the seminary to begin his studies, he met the faculty: Dr. James Grier, the seminary president and teacher of theology and preaching, Dr. David McClanahan, teacher of Old Testament literature and criticism, Dr. John McNaughen, teacher of New Testament literature and criticism, and Dr. John Wilson, teacher of church history and pastoral theology and the seminary librarian. He promised them, as was required of all entering students, that he would diligently attend all the instructions of his professors, that he would promptly comply with all lawful requirements of the faculty and be subject to their authority, that he would honestly conform to all the regulations of the seminary and not propagate any opinions in opposition to the standards of the United Presbyterian Church.

The wind off the three rivers blew cold in December whenever one walked outdoors. The town of Allegheny sat at the point where the Allegheny and the Monongahela flowed into the Ohio, and while the seminary was not right on the banks of any of the rivers, the chill wind pierced a woolen coat pretty quickly. Robert had expected that the winter would be milder here than back home on the farm in upstate New York, just as it had been in Princeton. Still, there was no large body of water near Princeton, and the damp made a difference.

It was good to be at Allegheny Seminary. The library was not as large as Princeton's had been; still, at five thousand volumes dedicated to biblical and theological studies, it was impressive. In his second year, enrollment was the seminary's largest so far, with eighty-nine enrolled. Two of his fellow middlers were men Robert had known as an undergraduate. Clarence Manor had been a freshman with him at Westminster, and William Jamison had graduated with him from Princeton. Both were fine company and were among the people Robert enjoyed discussing theology with and even drilling Greek. New Testament Greek was pretty different from classical, and daily translation took careful attention. Robert decided early in the spring term of his first year that daily translation was a practice that should not end when seminary ended. How could a man hope to understand the text if he did not keep up his language skills in ministry? Since then, he had faithfully followed the practice of translating a chapter from the Greek New Testament each day. This year, he was working to master Hebrew well enough to translate a chapter from the Old Testament each day, as well.

The course outline was rigorous and fascinating at the same time. Systematic theology included study of the creation of the world, evolutionary theories, providence, the constitution of the soul (including the conscience and the will), the covenant of works, the nature of sin and the sin of Adam (which got us all into the mess of sin), the covenant of grace, Christ's person, and acts of mediation on our behalf. There were Old Testament and New Testament literature and criticism, church history, speaking, and preaching, each required in each term, with the emphasis on the biblical material different each year. In addition, each class received weekly instruction in experimental religion, which turned out to be the practice of worship in the church and on the mission field, with practical examples of varieties of ways of structuring the worship service. During the course of the three years, one must also master Presbyterian order and discipline through study of the book and attend lectures on the formation and history of the canons of the Old and New Testaments, and on Christian missions and Christian Apologetics, the reasoned study of the historical and evidence bases of Christianity to prepare one to defend the faith against objections. In the senior year, everyone took a course in pastoral theology.

Robert tried not to think too much about the whole course of study. It was overwhelming to realize everything that one needed to learn in just three short years to be prepared for ministry. At the same time, it was good to know that the curriculum had been well thought out and planned so that each year's study built on what had been taught the previous year and added depth and breadth to understanding. Already in this first half of his seminary years, Robert had learned much about missions. Who knew that the gospel had first gone to India in the first century with the apostle Thomas? If doubting Thomas could be an effective missionary when the Spirit gave him power to preach, there was perhaps hope for a fellow from New York farm country. He could see that the lectures on missions and on apologetics would be powerfully important for his understanding of the work he hoped to do. Mission work was a challenge in cultures where pagan religions had been dominant for centuries.

The news out of China had rocked the campus with the reminder that mission was also dangerous. Two German missionaries had been killed in China earlier in the year, and now the Germans were building a naval base there to defend the efforts of the church in Tsing Dao. Dinner table discussion the night that news came centered on what American missionaries could expect, since here, unlike Germany, there is no state-supported church.

***

The summer between first and second year (or junior and middler year, as they were called), Robert had stayed in Pittsburgh rather than incurring the expense of traveling home. He received permission to stay in Hanna Hall, the seminary dormitory, at a rate of eight dollars for a suite of rooms, shared with another student remaining for the summer. It was no small amount for a seminarian on half-stipend, but far more reasonable than a train ticket home and back. The opportunity to serve as a student minister under supervision was not to be missed. He was eager to gain practical experience, applying those things he had been learning in the classroom.

The dormitory was a pleasant place to live. Each suite had both a study and a bedroom. Light and ventilation were good and healthful. The building was oriented east and west, designed so that each suite of rooms received one half-day of sunlight. As had been true of his accommodations in Princeton, there was an indoor water closet, and unlike Princeton, where one showered in the gym, each hall had a tub with running water for bathing. Robert smiled every time he thought how envious Charlie would be that there was no privy to clean out, though he was always careful not to mention the arrangements in letters home. During the year, there was no cost for housing, but summer was different. Summer was also different in the fact that the committee of ladies appointed by the board of directors did not inspect the rooms monthly, as they did during the academic year. Not that Robert was slovenly in his habits; Mother and his sisters had taught him enough housekeeping skills to keep his things in order. Still, it had been nice to know that no ladies would be parading through during the months he was away from campus, serving in student ministry.

As was true for most students following the first year, Robert had been assigned to provide general missionary work for an unevangelized area near the seminary. His work introduced him to families down near the river; these men worked on the barges and steamships that kept the three rivers busy. He had spent much of his time organizing the children of the neighborhood in games and teaching them Bible stories. The children seemed to enjoy the activities. His stories of heroes of the Bible kept their interest, and he had had good success teaching the older ones the first part of the shorter catechism. On Sundays, he visited with their parents in the neighborhood and offered out-of-door worship service in the evening for those who would come. It was hard to say whether they came more out of desire for nurture in the faith or for the free entertainment; still, some came weekly, and as the summer progressed, he was welcomed into many homes to bless new babies and to visit with the sick and aged.

That summer, Robert learned a great deal about ministry beyond preaching and teaching. More than that, he had learned a great deal about the lives of workers whose days were shaped by some boss's schedule far more than by their own design. Farm work was hard, but a man could set his schedule according to what he knew needed to be done, and if he managed well, he and his family could prosper. Last summer, Robert had gotten to know people who had few prospects for a future any different from the present, which was pretty impoverished.

For his own spiritual nurture, Robert worshipped with a congregation of the Presbyterian Church in North America in Allegheny during his first year in seminary. During that year, one of the guest lecturers on missions was from the East Liberty Church, which had a strong commitment to foreign mission. Robert visited East Liberty because he wanted to learn more about that commitment. The East Liberty area of Pittsburgh was as prosperous economically as Allegheny. The congregation had many young people near Robert's own age, and he was grateful for the opportunity to meet some people beyond the seminary community.

One young woman in particular stood out in his memory of those he met. Maud Pollock was the daughter of a greengrocer in the East Liberty neighborhood. Her father, William Pollock, was an admirable man in many ways, Robert had discovered. He served on the Central Board of Education, having first been elected in 1877 when Maud was only five. Now, in the late '90s, he was chairman of the Committee on Teachers and Salaries. Education was very important to Pollock. His five children all received an education beyond high school. Maud and her sisters, Nan and Nell, were trained as teachers. At present, having finished her course, Maud was teaching children at the Good Hope Mission School in Pittsburgh.

Now in the winter of his middler year, Robert was occasionally invited to dine with the Pollock family. He was delighted to know the family and especially Maud. It was a joy to know a young woman whose passion for education and for mission seemed to match his own. He prayed that if God willed it, he might share his life with such a woman. He knew that such thoughts were perhaps premature. For Maud to leave her close-knit family and the work she so enjoyed would be a difficult thing. Time would tell them whether they were in God's will for each other. In the meantime, the company was very pleasant, not only Maud's but that of her family, as well.

***

Returning for his senior year, Robert stopped in Philadelphia to apply for foreign mission service, hoping to be appointed right out of seminary. At the end of his interview, he was told that his application could not be approved at that time. Some time in a local church could help him develop understanding of pastoral work and some practical skills that would be of real value in the mission field. Robert received the news with disappointment but saw it as wise counsel; he took advantage of opportunities to interview with search committees that came to the seminary to interview potential candidates during the year. The church in Crosswell, Michigan, called him to be its pastor, knowing full well that he would not be with them long because of his calling to mission service. Being so far from Maud would not be

A PROMISED LIFE

pleasant, but he could fulfill the board's requirement and reapply for mission service once his term in Crosswell was complete. Robert came to graduation with a call in hand and left for Michigan with his bachelor of divinity degree to be ordained and begin in ministry.

CHAPTER

3

The Work Begins: 1900–1901

All through the years, Mother's prayers and Father's instruction had indicated there was more than farming in Robert's future. The whole congregation and community had always known he was headed for the ministry, and all the family knew it too. Uncle John and Uncle Samuel had offered help and advice on prayer and study as far back as Robert could remember. Now looking back, the years of working in the fields beside Davey and Charles, flying down snowy hills on their skis when winter blanketed those fields in snow, flew by as quickly as a winter afternoon. Princeton had been far from the farm, not as far geographically as New Wilmington, but much farther in terms of the way people thought and believed. Among those city folk and liberal thinkers, Robert had felt a stranger, almost as if he were surrounded by heathens. Their childhood pastor had once written to Elizabeth of the folks in Nebraska, "So many who were once members of the church in the East are not Christians out here so far as outward show is concerned & do not identify themselves with the church."[4]

In New Jersey, Robert learned that you did not have to go all the way to Nebraska to find people like that. Westminster College had been much more like home, full of good North American Presbyterian faculty and students. It had been a good place to learn and become ready for the years of seminary ahead. Allegheny, the

A Promised Life

United Presbyterian Church in North America seminary, was just the right place to prepare for ministry. Many of his classmates had had the same passion for mission service that burned in Robert's heart. His teachers and the pastor of the church where he served his internship had encouraged Robert to offer himself for mission service. Maud had herself trained as a teacher; she wanted to go to the mission field with him to work alongside him in educational mission and to be his wife. The only setback was the Board of Mission Work itself. The board had denied Robert's application when he graduated from seminary, saying he needed some parish experience first. Surely the Lord's hand was in this, though it had been a great disappointment to be turned down at the time.

Now in May of 1900, Robert could see God's wisdom in his year in Croswell, Michigan. If in fact, as he and his mother had always firmly believed, God was calling him to foreign educational mission service, likely there was no better preparation than this work with Sunday school children and parents north of Detroit. He could only be grateful for the chance God had given him before he set out for the other side of the world to work with people even more unfamiliar than those folks in New Jersey. Whether the new application was accepted or not, Robert and Maud would be married in August.

He told Elizabeth:

> I expect you will all think I am a schemer to plan to make a visit when there is not much doing on the farm. The reason I planned it so was not to escape work but to keep out of the way. I do not think I could do much to help along, and I feared I should be a great drawback. The way George has no man, I might do good as a kind of chore boy but I fear I am not so fit for work as formerly, and coming from this cool place, I shall need to avoid the heat. I could probably walk as far as any of you in a day, but I expect I would prove poor help at oat harvest.
>
> Do not worry about my health. It has been good ever since I came here, and I expect it will be as this cool climate I find to be very bracing in summer. It

27

is about the same as you have. Tell Mother I often think of her and want her to get real strong before I bring her a new daughter-in-law. I judge from your letter that Father is working as usual. I guess he and Mother had to work better than some of their children – this does not mean you.

With love to all, Robert Maxwell[5]

The work gave Robert plenty of opportunity for physical exercise. Writing in June, he described his travels around both to tend to his own parish and to fulfill obligations to other pastors:

A physician who attended me died Mon. morning. His wife, Mrs. Acurand, wished me to conduct the funeral services, but I was north and received word a day too late so I stayed for prayer meeting at Erskine and preached last night at Curaker. Tuesday when I should have called at P.A. I was hustling about making seventeen calls and riding bicycle 18 miles besides matters, too. Wed., I did no calling hardly but rode about fifteen miles and walked four or five. Yesterday the ground was muddy in morning and afternoon before I had gone a mile I broke Bicycle, a very trifling break but sufficient to prevent me riding, so I walked thirteen miles to Curaker, covering in all about 17 miles on foot besides the miles I rode. I am sure tired tonight but being able to walk off 11 miles without a rest shows that I am not particularly weak or infirm.[6]

Elizabeth was faithful to keep her brother apprised of news from home. She wrote proudly that Charlie had attended the temperance meeting and that she was keeping busy with nieces and nephews but finding time for the women's prayer meeting. She mentioned a conversation with Frank Dobbins, Robert's high school classmate, and Robert had to tease in return, "You must appear quite young or else he

A Promised Life

is inexperienced when he set you down as younger than Charles. Tell Charles he will have to shape up a little or he will become a regular mossback if he appears older than you. If I recall right there must be 6, 8 or 10 years difference in your ages?"[7]

Between her repeated illnesses and place in the middle of the family, so that there were always young ones to help tend, Elizabeth had not found time to seriously court or think of marriage. It did not stop her enjoying the company of young men. Truly, she was a faithful daughter and sister. While her brothers tended the crops, she tended the young turkeys they were raising, racing out to gather them in if rain threatened. The turkeys were a new try at a cash crop for the fall, since it seemed everyone wanted turkey for Thanksgiving tables. Robert worried that her fragile health would not stand up to the stresses of active farm life. Elizabeth had pledged herself to help raise his support when he was accepted for mission service, to manage his stateside accounts and business, and see to the children he and Maud hoped they would have to someday send home for schooling. She would be the third partner in this mission endeavor, a partner he and Maud would be grateful to rely on. Anticipating marriage and family was a joy but also a concern, knowing how little income the church provided.

He wrote to his sister, "I get quite discouraged in my effort to see how two can live on $700 a year, but on the other hand I do not think I can stay here single for any great length of time. Pray God to deliver me from this horrible dilemma."[8]

***

Elizabeth Paige Maxwell McRight

Robert traveled to Pittsburgh for his wedding, and Robert and Maud were married on August 14, 1900, with Maud's family, including sisters Nan and Nell and brother Robert, in attendance. Following the wedding, they had a happy visit with the Pollock family and enjoyed the sights in Pittsburgh, the scene of their courtship during Robert's seminary days. The pleasure of these days was sharpened by anticipation of news from the mission board meeting. Finally, word came from Dr. James Barr that Robert had been approved to serve on the mission field in India. Oh, such joy. The long-anticipated hope was finally fulfilled, and Robert and Maud would be off to India in October. Plans now included a trip to Michigan to settle things there before heading east to visit with the Maxwells in Cambridge and then on to New York and the boat. Robert and Maud allowed themselves ten days for goodbyes with the Croswell congregation, packing up Robert's household goods, and arranging to ship things to the farm in New York. Robert wrote to ask Elizabeth to keep their visit to the family just in the family as much as possible, since by the time they arrived, they would be "an old married couple" and would want to spend their time visiting with family. It was Maud's time to get to know her new family, and it would be seven years before they saw them again.

Back in Pittsburgh, Maud attended to her packing for India

with her mother and sisters' help. Her trunks went with the couple as they traveled. At the farm, once things arrived from Croswell, Robert divided what would go with them and what would remain in New York. Charlie became the owner of Robert's bicycle. Elizabeth was glad to take on the distribution of Robert's Michigan winter clothing, which would have no place in India's climate. The month of September quickly passed by, with preparations for the new life in India and visits with the various members of the Maxwell and Telford families. The congregation in East Greenwich was very proud of their former member, bound for the mission field with his bride, and many prayers for their work were shared, with promises to hold them up in prayer both in their travels and in their service that God would bless their efforts on His behalf.

At last the time to be away came. Robert's brother, George, hitched up his horses, loaded up the trunks and the couple, and headed for the train in Cambridge. They visited with Mrs. John Hunt on the train and had a restful trip to the city and the seagoing vessel that would take them to Europe. Dr. Barr, who had himself been a missionary to the very area where they were going, met them at their hotel and accompanied them on a shopping expedition. The next day, he went with them to Brooklyn to the ship, introduced them to the captain, and stayed with them, visiting until time for the ship to sail. George saw them and their goods on board and toured the ship with them. Then he said his own goodbyes and headed back to his farm. Dr. Barr stayed with the couple until last call for visitors to leave. Just before he left them, Dr. Barr led them in prayer for this grand voyage and calling. When he left, they waved to him on shore until they could no longer see him and then watched the Statue of Liberty recede from view. Finally, when all around was sea, they opened letters and packages from friends that had been waiting in their cabin when they arrived. Among them were an American flag sent by Aunt Barbara and her girls, a special treasure since they had neglected to buy one, and a testimonial from the Good Hope Mission, which wished Maud well in her new work, as well as letters from both Cambridge and Pittsburgh families.

***

VOYAGE TO INDIA

On September 15, 1900, Robert and Maud Maxwell set sail for their new life together in the north of what was then India (and is now Pakistan), not knowing any of the languages of the region to which they were going, except for the English spoken by educated Indians as well as by the British who ruled that part of the empire. They did not know which town they'd be assigned to. They knew they were going to teach, and Robert would preach, and there would be much to learn in the process, especially in the beginning.

The couple had traveled some, Robert more than Maud, but this trip was not like anything they had experienced before. Different people, different cultures, many new sights, sounds, and smells made the whole journey an amazing experience from day one. They were delighted with each other and delighted to share the adventure. Happy and confident in themselves, they soon made happy acquaintance of fellow travelers and crew alike and wrote to Elizabeth all along the way, to share the adventure with the folks at home.

Not all was lighthearted fun. Beginning with the fish course at dinner the first night, Maud discovered that seasickness made the journey much less fun. Then, two days out a storm at sea arose. Robert wrote to Elizabeth:

> A storm at sea can be better imagined than described. The good ship rolled from side to side more than a cradle. Along the passage where we were was a cushioned seat, and as Maud was less sick when lying she lay on the seat, and I sat on the edge with both feet against the railing which ran along within 3 feet of the seat to hold her on. Before when the motion had been much less violent, she had rolled off, and Tuesday when the waves washed over the top of the whole and every timber creaked, it was with some difficulty that I kept her from rolling off onto the floor. The floor where we were and the floor of the promenade deck where we usually sit are about level, and waves broke against the side of the cabin

repeatedly with great force, occasionally going clear over the railing, the top of which is probably 25 feet above the usual water line.

Some who persisted in remaining on deck were pitched out of their chairs and rolled over the deck against the outside railing. One a woman who was with difficulty forced into the rear smoking room in which was about 6 inches of water; she is now called the smoking lady. The stairway leading from the promenade deck up to the bridge where the officers look out was torn away on the windward side. Both chimneys probably 10 feet in diameter were torn loose at the bottom and swayed to and fro until stayed next morning.

One of the lifeboats which hang out over the rail but above the level of the promenade deck was lifted so as to take one of the davits out of its socket. The davit is of iron perhaps 15 feet long and 4 inches in diameter. The boom which kept the lifeboat from swinging in on deck is broken almost in two. And it is a stick about 6 or 8 inches in diameter. Another lifeboat which sits on deck was dinged as if struck with a small pile driver. While the storm lasted, we were regaled by a medley of sounds. The creaking of timbers, the falling of the stairs, the rushing waters, the violent wrath of the ventilator which let in water occasionally, the breaking of dozens of plates and other dishes, and the shouts of frightened women at each peculiarly violent lurch of the ship were enough to keep us awake if the ship had been riding smoothly.

Once after a violent shaking, we were quite alarmed by seeing smoke rising through an open ventilator, but by smell, we were reassured it was only the steam of scorching food, which we agree had probably been spilled from an overturned kettle. At dinner we suffered from the result, as our 10-course dinner was reduced to four or five courses. During the night after the storm, the vessel rolled enough to keep Maud awake some, but I slept very well, and as we were in the same bed, she was less nervous.

Next morning, sky was cloudy but the sea was much quieter, and yesterday we had sunshine all day and have today thus far... Maud was considerably reduced as vomiting does not agree with her, but now all are feeling fine and expect to finish the voyage in triumph. The Capt. assures us that we get only one such storm on a ticket, and we need not expect another. Wednesday a multitude of porpoises played alongside and in front of the ship for a few miles and provided a delightful relaxation after the storm. They jump clear out of the water about a foot and glide along for six or seven feet before they plunge in again. They seemed to be racing with the ship. They were about 2 feet long and perhaps ten in circumference. [9]

On September 25, the ship passed through the Strait of Gibraltar into the Mediterranean Sea. Robert wrote to Elizabeth that once they were off the Atlantic, he no longer worried about their safety. A long letter followed, describing the sights in Gibraltar, including the bull ring, constant beggars, and the use of donkeys as beasts of burden. This last sight was new to Robert and Maud, though later it would become a daily occurrence, as donkeys passed their compound loaded with bricks, sand, and other supplies for road building. Of this first encounter, Robert wrote:

Instead of horses to move things they use donkeys. They drive some like a sheep, except they get a little more familiar and whack them on the side of the head when they want them to turn in the opposite direction. They wear very little barriers except a wicker work saddle, something like two-pointed hats woven together along the brim or one side all the brim on the other side cut off. The two points hanging on each side halfway down the side of the donkey are filled with charcoal or grapes as the case may be. One ridiculous load we saw was a donkey loaded with long bamboo poles like fighting rods. They hung down before and behind the donkey, but he patiently plodded along under them. From the grapes I saw loaded on some of the beasts, I think they could carry 2 bushels of potatoes on each side. The people mostly ride behind or on the backs of horses, but the poor donkeys have to carry the burdens.[10]

After a brief day's tour, it was back to sailing, as they headed for Genoa and on to Trieste and the ship that would take them to India. Sailing was much calmer now, and daytime and evening were taken up with games with the other passengers. Robert described deck shuffleboard to his sister, complete with drawings of the board and paddle. He also confessed to her that he and Maud had entertained themselves privately by making disparaging comments about some of the passengers the ship picked up at Gibraltar. It was their first encounter with people who did not speak any English and who looked strange to a couple accustomed to American dress and manners. Robert was embarrassed at himself and realized that he and Maud would need to be more accepting of those whose ways were different from their own if they were to be effective in their mission work.

When they arrived in Naples, they were unable to leave the boat due to the presence of two anarchists among them. The captain had cabled ahead from Gibraltar, and there were police boats waiting in the harbor to relieve them of the two men. The boat sailed on to Genoa, where they transferred to a narrow boat, twelve feet by six. In it overnight, the women slept in one cabin with eight berths, and the men separately. They arrived in Trieste, near present-day Slovenia, on October 2. After two days in Trieste, they once more set sail on a larger vessel bound through the Suez Canal for India.

Neither wrote home about that part of the journey. One can only imagine how it must have been for them to see the sights on that part of the voyage: they passed ancient terraces and may well have stopped to wonder whether their Lord had seen those same terraces during his time as a tiny child in Egypt. They traveled on through the Red Sea that Moses crossed so many thousand years before them and saw Mount Sinai in the distance, across the red and rocky desert. At long last, they came to the Indian Ocean and crossed to the land that would become home, the birthplace of four of their five children.

They arrived at Bombay, now Mumbai, on a Wednesday evening after about a month at sea and disembarked the middle of the next morning. They bought tickets to Sialkot and secured a compartment with sleeping accommodations for five through to Sudhiarra. They changed English and French gold into rupees, at about thirty-three cents on the pound, bought some things, and booked their trunks to Sialkot. After seeing very little of the city, which seemed especially dirty and noisy, they left on the train at 8:30 p.m. A Miss Crenshaw and Miss Greenfield were traveling companions and also Dr. Brandon, who booked in another compartment, where he slept with some other men but spent the day with the party, as they had seating accommodation for nine. On the way, they took on a train car that carried a soda water man, and the edibles were furnished as they went. Pieces of bread, canned sardines, nine rupees' worth of fruit jellies, and tea that Miss Greenfield brewed made a quite sufficient supply. Tea was often brought to the car window, as well as water buffalo's milk, and big leather water bottles full of tepid water were carried about by railroad porters.

The scenery was beautiful and varied. Great stretches were jungle, but some of the way, they watched the farmers sowing their crops. The whole unplowed surface was bright green and was in marked contrast with what some of the new arrivals had expected. The rains were abundant, and several bridges along the route had been carried away. The US Presbyterian party left Itarsi about noon Friday, but Miss Greenfield, who acted as the Maxwells' guide, remained with them until Saturday evening, when they arrived at Sudhiarra, her home station. There she provided hospitality over Sabbath. They were four in one house, and despite two lizards in each of the rooms and white ants working in the walls and laying mud in many places, Robert and Maud slept soundly and got a good rest overnight.

They attended Sunday school, an English class, and preaching in Punjabi, and in the evening, Robert spoke briefly from First Timothy 6:12, and others followed with remarks and welcomed the Maxwells. Miss Greenfield had once been under an English Mission Society, but by the time Robert and Maud arrived, she worked on her own, as the society was defunct. All were very kind. Dr. Wherry showed them about the industrial school there and gave them some friendly advice. They left on the Monday morning train and proceeded on their journey. They telegraphed to Samuel Martin to expect them in the evening, and after changing trains twice, they arrived, but much to their surprise, they found no one they knew, and people who spoke English seemed rather scarce. They managed to hire a taxi cart and found an English-speaking individual who directed the driver to take them to the headmaster of the school, who would tell them about the North American Presbyterian Mission. They drove to him, and he kindly directed the driver to proceed to Rev. Samuel Martin, stating, however, that Dr. Martin was at church.

They proceeded just the same and stopped before a house, where Robert jumped out, and almost before he knocked, a woman asked who was there. Robert replied, and she said she was Mrs. Ballantyne and asked them to wait. It was about ten, as their train had been late. After a long wait, Mrs. Ballantyne came out and welcomed the Maxwells as people are seldom welcomed in America. She said she felt favored in being first to entertain them and waited anxiously for the return of her husband and the rest, who had been attending the annual meeting, which began on Friday. It seemed all providential. Mrs. Ballantyne, too, would have been away from home, but her oldest girl had tired, and she had brought her home.

If she had not been home, Robert knew they could probably have driven three miles more to the North Compound, where Dr. Anderson lived. The Ballantynes and Martins were in the South Compound of the mission. Rev. Robert Cummings and his wife had arrived earlier, along with two ladies who were going to Wazirabad. Telegrams were received on Friday, one for the Maxwells, saying, "Anderson arrived at Port Said. Expect from Tuesday morning," and one for Anderson. Their own telegram sent Monday came only after they had arrived. Even Tuesday morning, when the association met at 7:15 so as to adjourn to go and meet Anderson and them at the station, a telegram was read from the ladies who went on to Wazirabad, saying all had arrived, so most went to the nine o'clock train, expecting to receive them. The Maxwells were beginning to learn that communication and transportation operated differently on the subcontinent of India than at home.

The next morning, they slept late and were driven to the train to meet Anderson, but someone came, saying that there was a scheme afoot to get the old missionaries to the North Compound before the new ones, so Rev. Ballantyne got out of the dog cart, leaving his wife and child, and climbed into the cart with Robert and Maud, and they started for the mission before the train pulled in. They ran the horses fast part of the way and came up just as the committee appointed to welcome them drove up from the train. It was quite exciting. Dr. Anderson arrived considerably later, and the fact that he got left in Egypt and did not overtake the green travelers fueled many jokes.

When they arrived at the mission, newspapers and a letter from Elizabeth were waiting. From the letter, Robert learned of the distribution of his clothing left in her charge to give away. He was especially glad to know that his heavy black suit had gone to a black man, one of the many migrating from the South to find factory work in Northern cities. The suit went with donations from his home church to support that work.

Elizabeth had written of the cost of butter, and her words made Robert smile, as he thought of the different worlds they now occupied. In India, the butter was white as milk and without salt. It was made from the milk of the water buffalo, a very ugly-looking animal nearly devoid of hair and with horns pointing in the wrong direction.

It was good to know they were remembered in the family's prayers. They depended on them, and they were so free from fear and anxiety, they felt sure God had heard. Robert was also glad to learn that the furniture had arrived. He knew from past experience that Elizabeth did business with prudence and dispatch. He wondered how she would make out in the turkey business at Thanksgiving. Thoughts of that time a month away, when Robert's letter to her would arrive, reminded him to include instructions to Charlie for the winter storing and care of the bicycle so that it did not rust, while there was snow on the ground to prevent its use.

The newspapers told of the situation in China, where the United States, Britain, and Japan had sent troops to rescue people and put down the Boxer Rebellion. The situation in Beijing was particularly harsh, with many innocent Chinese deprived of their property and injured. Robert was astonished to see the pictures on the front page. They got the Midland newspaper, *Christian Instructor,* and *County Post.* Seeing the photos of the conflict in China, Robert could understand his father's concern about their own welfare, which Elizabeth referred to in her letter. The papers also confirmed the importance of the work to which Robert and Maud were assigned. Literacy in 1900 was projected to be 90 percent in Britain, between 70 and 90 percent in the United States, and less than 30 percent in India and other parts of Asia and Africa.

Saturday night, a reception was given for the Maxwells. On the bulletin board was a drawing representing two couples in advance, Cummings and Maxwells, with Anderson pursuing. Rev. J. Howard Martin, who had been in the field since 1888, presided and made a welcome address, to which Robert responded. His wife, Josephine Martin, gave a recitation; Dr. Gordon and Miss Dickey did a solo each; and Rev. David Gordon, Mrs. Ballantyne, and May Caldwell with Rev. Martin formed a quartet. Rev. Youngsten of the Scottish Mission led closing worship. There were probably seventy-five present. Robert wore preaching clothes and Maud her white dress. Rev. Gordon and Rev. Ballantyne remembered the Maxwells' house in Cambridge, but only after effort of the whole day did Rev. Ballantyne recall Robert, a slightly humbling experience. It turned out Mrs. Ballantyne was an old chum of his mother's.

They were assigned to Rawalpindi for the first six months, during which their time would be taken up mostly with language studies. Rev. and Mrs. W. B. Anderson, Rev. and Mrs. John McConnelee, Mrs. Robert McClure, whose husband had died in the mission the year before, and Josephine White, an early educational missionary, were all in the North Compound with them. Robert hoped he could do something in Gordon Memorial College or the YMCA once he had the necessary language skills. Dr. Anderson had been trying to get them there, and it was Robert's choice, of all the places, he thought.

Jhelum, where T. F. Scott was, lay between Sialkot and Rawalpindi, and the Maxwells accepted his invitation to spend a week or two with them. Mrs. Scott and the girls came from the hills while they were still in Sialkot, and they found the children delightful. Thus, the adventure began.

CHAPTER
4

Mission Work in India and Pakistan

The India in which Robert and Maud began to work was part of the British Empire. Organized British interest in India began in 1600, with the establishment of the British East India Company. The company grew quickly and came to account for half of the world's trade, especially in commodities like cotton, silk, indigo dye, salt, tea, and opium. The subcontinent of India was a series of independent principalities before the 1600s. In 1757, with the decisive defeat of the ruler of Bengal and his allies from the French East India Company by the British, with support from leaders of other principalities who marshalled their forces to the fight, the company began to control large portions of India. It established its own armies and gained administrative responsibilities over increasing areas.

This lasted until 1856, when rebellion broke out in several principalities in northern central India. Known as the First Indian War of Independence and the Sepoy Rebellion, among other names, this disturbance ultimately led to the dissolution of the East India Company and the establishment of direct British government control of India in 1858. Charles Canning was appointed governor-general of India in early 1856. He was a man of strong common sense and sound practical judgment; he led with an attitude of conciliation toward the native princes and a policy of promoting measures to work toward the betterment of the people. Following the rebellion, he was appointed the first viceroy of India. He established a more liberal policy and a sounder financial system than before the rebellion and left the people more contented than they were before. He resisted British public sentiment to punish all the rebel leaders severely and offered clemency to all soldiers and officers who had disbanded and returned home at the end of hostilities, punishing only those who had mutinied and killed their officers and English civilians. He developed departments of government with both British and native Indian members, encouraged the development of the railway system, provided famine relief, and established schools of higher education in Madras, Bombay, and Calcutta. In a relatively short four years, all this helped calm the rebellion and led to acceptance of British colonialism. Canning resigned following the death of his wife in 1861.

Christianity came to India in the first century AD, according to tradition, with the visit of the apostle Thomas. Thomist churches still exist in India. In 1591, the first Christians known to be in the north of India were received in the court of Emperor Akbar in Lahore. They were Jesuit Catholic priests and a lay brother from Goa, a port city in the south of India on the Arabian Sea and the first center of Catholicism in the Portuguese occupation of India. Priests accompanied Akbar in his Kabul campaign. The later Afghan invaders of the area treated the Christian community well. By 1600, there were ninety-six converts to Christianity in Lahore. Two generations later, the emperor was hostile to Christianity; all the churches in the Lahore region were destroyed, and the Catholic community resettled in Agra. In the time of the Sikh rule in the Punjab, there was an active Christian presence. The first Protestant missionaries to Lahore, Rev. and Mrs. John Lowrie, Presbyterians, were invited to open a school, but due to Lowrie's health, that was not possible.

The Protestant agencies in what is now Pakistan were the Anglican Church Missionary Society, based in London, the United Presbyterians in North America, the Church of Scotland, the United Methodist Church USA, the Salvation Army, the Associate Reformed Presbyterian Church of the USA, the Brethren Churches, the Danish Pathera Mission, Seventh-Day Adventists, the Church Missionary Society of Australia and New Zealand, the Worldwide Evangelistic

Crusade, the Afghan Border Crusade, and the Zenana Bible and Medical Mission. Most groups concentrated in a particular area, where they established separate villages for new converts.

The Presbyterians adopted a church-centered approach. The goal was not to produce a branch of any of the Presbyterian churches from the United States but a national indigenous church with its own native leadership. Presbyterian missionary work in India began in earnest in 1854 with Dr. and Mrs. Andrew Gordon at the Sialkot mission. The work later spread to eastern parts of the Punjab, including stations at Zafarwal (1880), Pasmir (1884), and Badomali (1915). Mission stations in central and western India were established at Gujranwala (1863), Lahore (circa 1913), Sheikhupura (1923), Martinpur (1918), Sangla Hill (1901), Lyallpur (1895), and Sargodha (1905). Along the border of the Jhelum River, mission stations were founded at Rawalpindi (1856), Jhelum (1874), Campbellpur (1916), and Taxila (1921). Near the Kashmir border, stations were founded at Gurdaspur (1872), Pathankot (1882), and Dhariwal (1890).

Work in India, while primarily evangelistic in nature, was also geared towards medical and educational concerns. Missionaries were involved with the creation and supervision of numerous institutions, ranging from village schools and technical training centers to colleges, including Kinnaird College for Women and Gordon College in Rawalpindi and Foreman College in Lahore, and hospitals, including the Sialkot Memorial Hospital and United Christian Hospital, Lahore.[11]

The first evangelistic outreach was to the high castes. In 1872, there were forty-three adult baptisms. Members of one lower caste, the Megs, were attracted by Presbyterian efforts. By 1905, the Zafarwal congregation alone had sixty-five Meg converts. The largest impact of Presbyterian witness was in the Chuhras caste, beginning with one handicapped man. By 1935, all of his family had become Christian. By 1990, 90 percent of Christians in Pakistan traced their ancestry back to the Chuhras caste.

By 1935, the Sialkot mission congregations had forty-three thousand members, with native pastors and officers. The responsibility for evangelism belonged more and more to these congregations. The missionaries provided decreasing funds and educational support for leaders. It was clear that the time was coming when the nation would be independent, and the native church leaders wanted to assume responsibility for the ministry. Gordon College in Rawalpindi and the Theological Seminary in Gujranwala, both established and maintained for many years by the Sialkot mission, provided education to Indian and Pakistani men. The college offered education to men of all faiths, Christian, Muslim, Hindu, and Sikh. The seminary trained pastoral leaders for Indian and later Pakistani churches, including the United Presbyterian Church in Pakistan. By 1961 there were 145 self-sustaining congregations in the area that had been Sialkot Mission in seven presbyteries with a total of fifty-five thousand members among the hundred forty thousand Protestants in Pakistan.[12]

***

The first year in the field found the Maxwells settling into the mission community. Their interest was not confined to just the local scene. The ties between those in the field and those back home were strong. Life was lived in the awareness that death and illness were ever near. Missionary children often did not thrive in the tropics. The mother and daughters of the Scott family said their goodbyes to friends in India and returned to the States for the daughters to go to school. Robert and Maud knew that their loved ones, especially William Pollock and Margaret Maxwell, might well not be alive when they next were in the United States, William because of his advanced age and Margaret because of her frail health. The distance made the exchange of news especially precious.

Maud summed up the stress of adjusting to life on two continents in a note she appended to Robert's letter to Elizabeth on May 1, 1901:

> I do not know that I have any news. Robert has written two letters and has told you all. We are both well and enjoying ourselves in spite of the fact that it is so very warm. We shall be glad enough to get to the hills. We have been hearing very regularly for some weeks from home. They were in the middle of moving when Rob wrote. They were a little

disappointed about moving. They expected to get the house three or four days before they did. They were all well. They had another big fire in Pittsburgh. The exposition building this time. I am afraid so much of the town will be destroyed if they keep on that I will not know it when I get there. I'll promise to write more next. Just now another snake charmer has made his appearance. He assures us the snake he has will not bite. It is horrible enough anyway.[13]

They were learning languages and learning about the educational system at the same time. Maud did not yet know that she would be asked to direct a school. After watching an assembly at the one under Mrs. McClure's direction in February, she wrote to Elizabeth:

Well I wish you could have been with us at the exercises this morning. My but the girls were noisy. It would drive me crazy to teach school in India. It was bad enough at home, but this is ten, yes, a hundred times worse. Each teacher and each caller had a big stick in her hand, and when any of the girls would do anything, one of them would reach for her with the stick. Well it only made them worse. Mrs. Anderson sent one of the callers into another room and put down the curtain. As soon as Mrs. Anderson turned her back, the old woman came out again.

The girls sang something, they say it was the multiplication table. I suppose it was, but I know you would never recognize it. I did not, I am sure. Mrs. Anderson had taught them a song. The girls lost the tune before they started this morning, and it was awful. Poor Mrs. McClure was so nervous. I thought she would be ill.[14]

They were eager for news from the farm, especially since Margaret Maxwell was in failing health, and Elizabeth's letters asked for their prayers that she would recover.

In October, Maud wrote to Elizabeth that Emma Scott had written about Ella's death after she and her mother and sister arrived in the States. They were still feeling badly. Their new home did not have the same attraction for them anymore. Emma said they never realized that she was going to die, although they knew she was very ill.

It was never all doom and gloom, however. These were, after all, young men and women living in compounds of several families working together to share Christ's love with natives of a foreign land. In the same letter, Maud offered a glimpse of the creative energy they shared, for fun as well as for the work:

> We had a very nice time at Mrs. Martin's on Sat. We were there for breakfast and tea.
>
> Mr. Martin proposed that we start a paper called the *Dharmscote Recuperator.* Mr. Ballantine was Editor-in-chief and all the rest section editors. Each one had to prepare a paper. Robert had the weather report and had to tell what the weather should be. I had notes and news. Miss Hill had to write on the care of a husband. Her first point in the care of a husband was to get the husband. Miss Spencer wrote a poem on affections. It was very good. Dr. Johnson had the scientific page. She said some very comical things.[15]

Robert and Maud went to Dharmsala for the summer, which lasted until November, after their first months with the Anderson family. Dr. Sophia Johnson was the physician in that part of India, widely respected for the way she was teaching health practices to the native women as well as for her skills in keeping the missionaries relatively healthy. She was a Eurasian woman, born in India and educated at the American Mission School. She had married a Scottish civil engineer. In 1880, she and Miss Euphemia Gordon had started the first medical work in the Sialkot mission, with advice from a Hindu doctor. The mission was convinced that the Bible and good medical care were both ways to share God's love. In 1885, the two women closed the hospital and went to the Women's Medical College in Philadelphia, where they completed their medical training and were admitted to practice before returning to India to serve as doctors to the people there.[16]

Malaria was a constant threat to the missionary families. Even though he took quinine daily, Robert suffered from bouts with it. In her letter Christmas Day, 1901, Maud wrote to Elizabeth about Dr. Johnson: "Robert is not well today. When he arrived last night, his temperature was 102°. He is out today and just now his temperature is 100°. I'm glad he's here again. Dr. Johnson said she will be able to give him a complete overhauling before she lets him go again."[17]

News of the world and of the family arrived by ship, often after a month in transit. The newspaper on September 6, 1901, brought news of President McKinley's assassination. Robert commented to Elizabeth, "We have some daily papers forwarded from Pittsburg describing in detail the Pres.' assassination. It was a horrible thing but perhaps it will teach people to be less merciful to those who violate the laws of God and man and thus be a blessing in the end. It is not right to allow such people as Emma Cold and her associate to make addresses that stir men up to such deeds. She has been at large for years telling men to overthrow government as the way to be happy."[18]

Libby's letter, which arrived in the same packet, brought more family news. Anna Belle had delivered a son, named for his uncle, Robert, who wrote, "Tell Belle that I think the boy has a good name. There is a Presbyterian missionary out here by that name who is very highly spoken of."[19]

Mail was often delayed. At Christmas time, packages from the Pollocks were held in the dead letter office until someone could go claim them. They contained jewelry and so had to be signed for.

1902 brought the Maxwells in India a little one of their own. By this time, they were settled in their own rooms, though they took meals with the others in the compound, as was the custom, a sensible way to keep the need for cooks and kitchen staff to a minimum while allowing the missionaries to concentrate on their primary work of teaching and health services. In an undated letter to brother Charles sometime early in the year, Robert began with a lengthy paragraph comparing growing seasons and fuel sources in upstate New York and in India, one farmer's son to another. Then, he wrote:

This girl of ours is a little nicer than anything you ever saw. She sleeps very well and causes us very little trouble. She was awake some yesterday, and we just begin to realize how kind she has been to sleep so much other days. We have a woman here in Ayah's place because the first Ayah did not seem able to care for the child as well. Maud cannot carry her, and as Ayah and I carry her a good deal, she sometimes appears to think she should be carried. At night, she sleeps all the time. Only one night have I carried her and then only for about half an hour. She usually wakens once to get something to eat.[20]

Margaret, named for her grandmother, who had died in 1901, arrived in February and immediately became the darling of both her parents. When the baby was about six weeks old, Dr. Johnson released Maud from the birthing hospital in Dharmsala to return to Rawalpindi. Maud wrote to Elizabeth:

> You will see by this that I am here at last. It did seem to take a long time for me to get here. The journey down almost wore Margaret and me out. It was hard for Robert too, and Margaret and I did not make it any easier. The native women talk so much and so loud that they wakened her every time the train stopped. I could have shot some of them. She got very tired and cried, and I got nervous and cross. I cannot nurse her altogether but have to give her one bottle a day. I am sorry about it, but cannot help it. The ayah came with us; she's not going to remain however. We're trying to get a Christian ayah and her husband. They were in Mrs. Gordon's service and were both very good.
>
> Robert is going to Sangla Hill tomorrow. I do not know how I should get along without him; he is such a help in taking care of Margaret.

We have not had Margaret baptized yet but will have it done as soon as possible. We want Mr. Scott to baptize her. He will be here in two weeks, and I think we shall have it done then.[21]

The family was separated for weeks on end during the warm months, Robert at his work and studies in Punjabi and Maud in the cooler hill country with Margaret. In response to news of Charles beginning to court, Robert wrote to his sister, "I do not know that I ever felt better except of course when I'm living with my family. That is due to other things as well as health however as Charles will be telling you one of these days." [22] In another letter in June, he reported that all was well with Maud and Margaret up in the hills: "Maud has grown some thinner since I saw her she says but I think she still has some weight. She seems to think Margaret worthy of all attention. I think I shall stand a very poor show when I return to them. They will think there are no people but themselves."[23]

The joy of parenthood too soon turned to grief for the Maxwells, as for so many. Robert's October letter to Elizabeth tells the story:

Abergeldi Cottage, October 13, 1902
My dear Elizabeth,

Two letters came this morning and none last week. One is marked 11 of September at East Greenwich, and I suspect it was posted too late. We did not mourn much last week over the letter we did not receive, as our darling who was laughing until one week ago this evening died one week ago tomorrow morning, and we were thinking of her more than anything else. We visited her grave each day since except for Sabbath. It is now covered with cement, and when the marble slab is laid over it, we expect to return to the plains. John Holloway has been quite ill, and we set up until 1:40 last night with him. He has tonsillitis and liver trouble.

October 16

John is still alive, and they have at last come down in hope of benefiting him. We're coming down on our own account as Margaret's stone was placed in position this morning. We are not with them however as our tonga lost a wheel, and we had to wait while another was being brought 2 miles and missed the train. I am very tired having covered about 10 miles on foot some of it uphill but mostly in a hurry down as we had work after sending women off and were anxious to catch them.

We did not kiss Margaret the last time you asked us to. We had laid her in the ground about a week before. God has wonderfully sustained us in all our loneliness. He is very kind. Commend him to all who know him not. Your brother, Robert Maxwell[24]

All her life, Maud kept a tortoiseshell pin that spelled out Margaret's name that some loved one sent to the baby. She and Robert would be blessed with four sons and ten grandchildren. She loved all her grandchildren, but the girls had a special place in her heart as she watched us grow up healthy and strong.

CHAPTER
5

Rawalpindi and New York: 1902–1907

During their first summer in Dharmsala, Robert and Maud lived with the Andersons, and Robert began to work at Boys High School in Rawalpindi while he continued to study Urdu and Hindi. In addition to studying and working at the school, he visited the churches within bicycle riding distance of Rawalpindi and began to become familiar with the people and culture around him. In a letter to his father in April, Robert wrote:

> The people here as everywhere else are the most peculiar thing. Yesterday I was riding the bicycle, and the tire punctured so I had to come on foot, and I took a short cut between the bridges crossing the stream on stepping stones. As I was starting to cross I saw a woman of perhaps seventy with nothing on that I noticed taking a bath. Such things are not at all surprising to us anymore, and we allow men to work around the yard and to come in for worship with so little on that you would send them to jail for indecent exposure. They go about with sort of pantaloons which seem to be made on a band and come to the knees in front but cover very little of the back of the

leg. Some go on the street with only a shirt and loin cloth on and some with nothing except the loin cloth and a very small one at that. Fakirs usually go with many rags about them, but occasionally one is seen without anything but sacred ashes on him, and they are fat lustful looking fellows, too. Women usually dress so as to cover themselves very well though they look strange at all times in pants, but when they bathe in the rivers, they think that if they do expose themselves, it is pleasing to the gods.

The plow used here would cause your eyes to stand out with wonder. It is a straight piece with sometimes a piece of iron on the point, and this is fastened to a long, crooked stick which is attached to the yoke. The furrow is about three inches deep and the same in width. They plow very small divisions, and the poor oxen and buffaloes keep turning around. They go over it often, and after they have worked with the plow to their satisfaction, they take a plank or clod crusher and go over it a few times with that.

One day I was watching a man plow as I supposed, and Rev. Scott asked me if I had seen him drilling in grain. I told him that I had seen him plowing but he said he was sowing, and I watched him more carefully and saw that the handle of his plow was hollow and he was taking grain from a sack which hung from his neck and dropping the grain through the hollow handle into the earth. The drill and plow were so much alike that I could not distinguish between them for a little distance. To dig they do not use spade or shovel but a sort of hoe which resembles a shovel with the handle stuck through one edge of it like the old hoe used by the slaves except that the side edges of this are slightly curved.

For the work of shoveling or rather of moving broken stone, I have seen them use an instrument with broad flat tines something like a potato fork, but instead of one man using it, three were trying to work it; one held the handle and two pulled strings to move the load. It looked like boys tying to plow with a stick.

Recently we have had a box made, and the carpenters did the planing with jack planes, but instead of one man working it, one pushed and one pulled. The box is quite good now that it is done, but two men were at it for a week, though I should say that they were waiting on the blacksmith for part of the time and now his work is not finished or we would have sent the box off today. They work so cheaply that Europeans cannot at all compete with them, so we are likely to have many different workmen during our stay here. A Christian man did the dealing with them and watched that they did the work instead of stealing or leaving, or we would have had more trouble and worry. [25]

He wrote to Elizabeth in the summer of 1902 that he hoped to have enough skill in Urdu to be able to preach when the time for itinerating came around. In the meantime, he was learning about trust in a whole new way. Each time he preached, he had to depend on someone else to translate his sermon for him so that the congregation could understand it. He could only hope that the translator was being true to the sermon as he had crafted it. In January of 1903, Maud wrote that Robert had led prayer service in Urdu and was complimented by the pastor of the church, Gandu Mall, on his ability to speak the language. In the same letter, Maud noted that she would teach in the same girls' school in Rawalpindi that she could never imagine teaching in two years before.

In 1903, Robert was manager of the Boys High School in Rawalpindi. The principal of the school was native born. This followed the normal pattern in the mission of having a native-born person in charge of relationships with students and their parents and a missionary in charge of hiring of staff and management of the funds allocated to the school by the church and by the government of India. The first two principals with whom Robert worked seemed unsatisfactory to the mission for different reasons. The first was not prepared for the task, and the second committed fraud. There were many frustrations working with people who were not up to the responsibilities laid on them, but Robert felt the idea of shared leadership was exactly right in principle. He knew that the goal was an independent church and independent educational system, and that meant sharing leadership until full responsibility could be turned over to the Indian partners.

Robert dealt with hiring staff and settling any issues and squabbles that came up among them. In 1903, there was a faculty of ten, including Robert, who taught Bible. By the end of 1904, for the whole school, lower and upper schools and technical, there was a faculty of forty-two. Exams were conducted at the end of each year for the state by a team made up of an Englishman, a Hindu, and a Muslim man to make sure the boys were getting a good quality education. The school student population varied from year to year, chiefly due to illness. In 1903, the middle school had 320 students. In 1904, it was reduced to 216 because of fear of plague. Fifty boys were sent to schools in other areas, even though plague had not come to the region at that time. Plague was so severe in some areas that crops stood unharvested in the fields because owners had died and the people who remained were too afraid of the sickness to venture out to harvest, even when promised half of all they harvested. Robert made sure that Elizabeth kept up his subscription to *The Youth's Companion* for the boys in school so that they could have it for English reading pleasure. He noted there was no British publication like it that he knew. It was a joy to him to have boys in the school eager to learn and enjoy the community life. Even though they were younger, the boys reminded him of his own days at Princeton and the friendships he had made there.

Robert became quite active in all aspects of mission life. He rejoiced to see converts coming. He did itinerant preaching on Sundays, traveling as many as twenty-five miles on his bicycle. He attended annual conferences of the mission and took part in the ecclesiastical matters, investigating complaints against missionaries and pastors (including at least one complaint of adultery). He recognized that people are human and are subject to the same temptations to cheat and use each other no matter where they live.

In 1904, in a speech at the fifty-year anniversary of the mission, he wondered where it would be by the centennial and questioned whether mission work would still be needed. That same year, he sat the Urdu exam, which he had been scheduled to do shortly after Margaret died. He passed, and in August of that year, he joined Maud in the hills with their first son, young William Pollock, born August 18, 1903. He described it as the "perfect place" in a letter to Elizabeth after several months of separation from his wife and child. Pollock seemed to have inherited his mother's hazel eyes instead of the brown eyes of his father. Robert hoped he had inherited her gentle, loving way as well.

Maud was keenly aware that some at home in the States took exception to the missionaries having servants. She explained to Elizabeth that there were times when she could not deal with life in India without some help from native people, like the day a monkey followed them home, wrecked the bathroom, and climbed to the roof and threw down bricks until the houseboy finally got him off the roof and took him home to his owner.

Maud continued to teach at the girls' school and for a short time was in charge of the school. A growing family in a strange land took more and more of her attention. February of 1905 was a banner month, George Small, named for Grandfather Maxwell, joined the family. Robert purchased a used typewriter from Mr. Porter of the mission for one hundred dollars and noticed that it improved both the speed of his writing and the readability of what he wrote. In April of that year, Maud wrote to Elizabeth that an earthquake had destroyed all the houses used by the missionaries in Dharmsala, except for the cottage they used in the hot months, which had been extensively damaged. There was much loss of life among the native people because the narrow streets made it almost impossible to escape before buildings collapsed. Several missionaries also died.

Robert and Maud traveled through the Khyber Pass riding by

train to Peshawar and crossing into Afghanistan by horse cart as far as people were permitted to go. They saw a tribe of people called Kaffides, who lived in caves and recognized no government but were paid a subsidy by the English and Afghans to keep peace. These men helped in the Afghan war; one of the officers said if it had not been for them, the English would never have been successful. They saw the old forts and the new ones. The pass was only open twice a week, and people had to bring across all they wanted on the two days. They saw a thousand camels, hundreds of donkeys, and dozens of cattle. It reminded Maud of the Bible's reference to wealth in camels and how people travelled in Bible times. They saw the knives the Kaffides used. She noted there was a man called an emir at the head of affairs, and if he did not suit them, he was quickly dispatched. One of the Kaffide told Robert that they fought about two things: the boundaries and cattle. No mission work was possible among the people of Afghanistan, as the emir did not allow the Bible to be taught in his domain.

Finally, in 1905, a principal was hired at the Boys' School who worked in a happy partnership with Robert for the rest of his time there. The school grew strong and produced several classes of men who went on into the college and took their place in the work force as leaders.

Robert led his family as a loving but firm Christian father, and Maud was his devoted partner. The household had breakfast each morning after Robert continued the practice he had begun in seminary of translating a chapter from the Hebrew Old Testament and a chapter from the Greek New Testament. Once he arrived, he dispensed a dose of quinine to everyone in the house, family and staff. There would be no more losses to malaria like Margaret's, if he could help it. Robert drank tea only socially and did not take coffee. At breakfast and dinner, he would drink hot water. His explanation to the family was that he wanted to avoid stimulants. His children later wondered whether this was from religious belief. It may well have had as much to do with the fact that his attack of scarlet fever in the year before college left him with a heart murmur and arrhythmia, which troubled him when he was very tired.

Pollock and George were active little boys, with hair as blond as Margaret's had been. Packages from America were a great surprise, especially when they contained treats not available in India. Pollock's favorite was Nabisco wafers, which came in metal tins. When the wafers were finished, the tins made new wagons for him and George, with the addition of empty spools from mother's sewing box hammered in by Father or Futtah, the houseboy.

As that year progressed, plans were laid for the family's first sabbatical visit home to America; they would see the Pollocks in Pittsburgh and the Maxwells in Cambridge. Little George would meet the grandfather for whom he was named. Pollock would meet the Pollocks, though his grandfather, William Pollock, would not be there. He had died the year before his namesake was born.

Robert wanted to visit as many congregations as he could as they traveled to tell people about the important work they were doing in the hope of building support for the schools. Maud wanted to tell the story, too, but before they left for America, she knew that her public speaking would be limited. The family would add an American-born baby, and she would finally be able to welcome a new arrival with her mother and her sisters.

***

Robert and Maud's mission partner in the States, Elizabeth was unflagging in her support of the work, handling business matters and shipping requested goods as she was able. Only one item in her hand remains of the correspondence between New York and India, a copy of a speech she gave in 1906 to her presbytery's women's gathering to inspire contributions to the work:

> It will be three years in October since Robert Maxwell was appointed Manager of boys' High School in Rawalpindi where he still labors. This mission station is located on the main line of railway from Peshawar to Calcutta and 111 miles southeast of the former. It is one of the largest native cities of

the Punjab and contains a cantonment and a military garrison superior in size to any other in India.

The congregation in Rawalpindi has a handsome and substantial Church building located in one of the best places in the city and quite near the High School building. You may remember that both buildings were on the ground when the Mission property was purchased from the Presbyterians in 1891. Included in the school is what is called the Main School located in a prominent position just at the edge of the city and three branch schools—one in Gujar Khan, a distance of 40 miles by train, one in the midst of the city and one in the Cantonment Bazaar.

On account of the plague two years ago the attendance was reduced very much but has been increasing the past year, and while it is not up to the old standard yet, in April the enrollment of Main School was 593 of the branches 115, 100 and 70 respectively. The school is for heathen boys and is one of the largest in the Punjab. The annual expense of carrying on the school amounts to about 18,000 Rupees or $6,000 which all passes though the manager's hands and is paid out by him in small amounts of which a strict account is kept. This expense is covered by fees and government and municipal aid. The school is practically self-supporting; the cost of teaching Bible being the largest sum that is paid by the Mission. Provision is made for teaching the Bible or Bible truth in every class in the school. The smaller boys of the primary are usually taught some easy question book and Bible stories are related. The more advanced classes are required to purchase testaments or Bibles, and these are used as text books during the remainder of the school course. The aim of the managers is to bring the boys in contact with Bible truth every day of their school life. In addition to this regular Bible work is the compulsory chapel attendance lasting 20 minutes every day and the optional attendance at Sunday school every Sabbath morning.

In the Main School Sunday School there are nearly 100 enrolled, but not more than 30 or 40 attend regularly. In the branch Sunday schools, the attendance is better. The school course covers 10 years, but many are coming and going as in every school and do not complete the course. School opens each day at 6:30 and closes at 11:30, except in the hot season and then it opens and closes one half hour earlier.

The manager teaches Bible four periods of 45 minutes each day, except Saturday when they are 20 min. and Sabbath, when he teaches a class in the Sunday school and has a Bible Circle made up chiefly of men who teach in the school, and the latter study different books of the Bible.

So many of the boys finish school without making any profession of religion, some think that the school for heathen boys is a failure but in all kinds of mission work there are discouragements and the fruit is not ready so soon as we could wish. However, many think that the Word of God in time will convert those who are to be saved, and many are reached in school who could be reached in no other way as many of them are high caste.

They not only hear the Bible but are compelled to study it. Many of them are good students and get a pretty fair knowledge of it while in the school and correct views of Christianity, and most of the pupils become friends of the missionaries and give them valuable assistance in their village and other work.

There are only about one dozen Christian boys in the Main school and about the same proportion in the branch schools, but there are others who said they believed in Christ before their classmates but do not seem ready to have the wrath of their parents and friends.

There are 42 men teaching and more than one dozen servants. The manager engages the teachers, and it requires time and labor as suitable teachers are scarce and then sometimes they do not remain long. During the year, counting the changes and new teachers employed, enough men were engaged to fill every place, starting with all full staff they made enough appointments to fill them again. The Government is about to open several schools, and the teachers are anxious to get places in them as many of the Government positions entitle the occupants to pensions when they have become too old to serve longer.

So far as possible efforts are made to secure Christian teachers, and I believe at present there are 13 on the staff. About the 1st of May there was a change in Head-Master of the school. The new one is a man with little training and less experience but he has energy and is a professing Christian. He had worked in the school six months previous. The discipline of the school has improved and reports of his work are most encouraging.

Inspectors visit and examine the school, spending about one week. The school receives Government aid to the amount of $240 per month which is increased or diminished according to results. The school has a good reading room for the boys, and her field days correspond with ours.

The manager is Secretary of the Men's Educational Board which has the oversight of the Boys Schools in the Mission. He often conducts examinations in other schools, and they are called upon to attend to various matters in connection with the schools. The duties of the missionary are many and varied usually pleasant but some such experiences as the following are very trying.

Because of lack of funds and sufficient men to carry on the work properly, he was ordered by the Mission to reduce Gujar Khan School from a High School to a Middle School which compares with our Grammar schools. The men of the village plead with him until long after mid night not to do it and offered pledges according to their ability for its support if he would only continue the High School for the benefit of their children as they were too poor to send them away to school.

And the chief man of a neighboring village visited him different times commending the work done by the school and begging him to send a missionary to their village to carry on the same work, offering to give land for the Mission buildings and support to the work. He longed to have the boys of his village educated in our schools and was willing to have them taught the Christian religion.[26]

CHAPTER

6

Second Season: 1908–1915

Early in 1908, four Maxwells shipped out for a furlough year in America. Many changes had taken place in the world in the seven years since Robert and Maud originally sailed. In 1901, Victoria, Queen of England and Empress of India, died, and Edward VII was crowned. Two years later, he was named Emperor of India. The eight-nation alliance of the British Empire, Russia, France, Germany, Japan, the United States, Austria Hungary, and Italy put down the Boxer Rebellion, but Western relationships and Christian missions in China were never as strong as they had been before the war.

President McKinley's sending of American forces to the conflict began the twentieth-century shift to a stronger executive branch of power in the United States. In the same year that Queen Victoria died, President McKinley was shot dead, and Theodore Roosevelt became president of the United States. Communication possibilities expanded as the first Morse code was sent across the Atlantic. Britain got push back from the colonies in many parts of the world. The era of a British Empire where the sun never set was beginning to wane. In 1902, the Boers surrendered to the British in South Africa.

In the United States, laborers' demands for better working conditions reached a new high with a five-month coal strike, the

A PROMISED LIFE

longest ever. Ultimately, President Roosevelt appointed a commission to settle it, resulting in nine-hour workdays and increased wages. In 1903, transportation took on new dimensions. The Wright brothers launched the first successful human-powered airplane flight at Kitty Hawk, North Carolina, and Henry Ford marketed the first mass-produced automobiles. The Bolshevik party was established in Imperial Russia, the start of the movement that would result in the death of the tsar and the Bolshevik Revolution in 1917, which would usher in the Soviet Socialist Republic. 1904 saw Britain and France settle their international differences peacefully, and the opening of the first line of the New York subway. 1905 brought the completion of the Trans-Siberian Railway. That year, Albert Einstein, then a clerk in the patent office in Bern, Switzerland, developed the special theory of relativity. The 1907 financial panic in the United States created an economic uncertainty that had a direct impact on giving to world missions. That same year, at the second Hague Peace Conference, forty-six nations established ten conventions on rules of war, an agreement which would influence the way World War I was waged four years later.

It also saw riots across India. In the north, where a larger percentage of the population were Muslim, there was deep resentment that higher caste Hindus seemed to get all the government jobs and a growing sentiment among both Hindus and Muslims to overthrow British rule and take back the government for themselves, by force if necessary. The rioting reached Rawalpindi in May, fed by reports in the local papers of racial hatred. The mob burned the homes of two Anglo residents, looted the mission church, and smashed windows in many homes. Armed police dispersed the rioters and set a watch in the fortified town, but Robert and Maud feared for the safety of their family and their neighbors, including the schoolchildren.

When Maud, Robert, Pollock (four), and George (two) arrived in the States in 1908, they knew they would be a welcome sight to the families who had worried for their safety since the news reports of the year before. The family made their way to Pittsburgh so that Maud's mother, Caroline, could meet her grandsons and help their parents attend to them in the latter stages of Maud's pregnancy. While they were there, Robert visited churches and his seminary, sharing the story of mission work in the Punjab. He inspired students at the seminary with his talk of preaching to men and women who had never heard the gospel before. He spoke frankly about the amount of his time that was spent in administration of the school. It was not work that he had imagined in seminary would take up so much of his time, but the education and training for a trade the school offered gave boys a chance at a life different from following their fathers' trade: gathering wood and dung for fires and cleaning streets for a living. Robert was convinced that this schooling might be as effective a witness of God's loving care as any sermon he preached, and he said so whenever he spoke.

He was with his family to welcome the newest member, Robert Wallace, on June 28. Many people joined them in welcoming him. At twelve pounds at birth, Robert Wallace Maxwell had the distinction of being the largest baby born in the Pittsburgh area to that time. That record did not go unnoticed, and many hospital personnel and others passed by the nursery to see this wonder for themselves.

By the time they arrived at the Maxwell farm in the fall, photos show a happy, solid babe in the lap of his grandfather, George Maxwell, surrounded by his brothers and two Murdoch cousins. Because of the birth, the visit was extended a bit so that Robert and Maud could do the visiting they intended and thank the churches that sponsored their work in person. Those who heard them were amazed at their courage and calm as they responded to questions about the civil unrest in India.

Nine-year-old George Murdock, Anna Belle's son, thought Uncle Robert was the most impressive man of faith he had ever met and decided that his cousins would not be the last of the family to live in India. Years later when first his sister, Margaret, and then George himself went to join Robert on the mission field, he found fulfillment of that dream of service and adventure planted when he was a boy.

In the fall of 1909, the Maxwells returned to India on the SS *Moldavia*. Their speed on the Atlantic was twenty-one miles per hour, on the Mediterranean fifteen miles per hour, but only six miles per hour through the Suez Canal. Robert wrote to his father on October 7 while the ship passed through the Red Sea. He noted that "sometime in the night or early morning we crossed where the Israelites crossed the sea and for a few moments sometime today we are in sight of Mount Sinai but we are attending to the boys instead of looking around. Sinai was pointed out to us when we went out before. The rocks and soil have a reddish color and are exceedingly bare. There is no green thing in sight. Along the canal there are some green spots irrigated with water from the Nile. Even the city of Port Said is supplied in that way."[27]

The boys traveled well on the journey. Robert reported that Wallace had another tooth, and all slept well, though he had prickly heat and the older boys perspired profusely in their sleep. Maud and Robert felt grateful to God that their own children prospered. A dance scheduled for the night before Robert wrote had to be postponed when a child was found dead in the first-class salon. A very sick child in second class meant that Pollock and George must keep quieter than they liked to be. They reached the port of Aden in present-day Yemen two days later and from there on to Bombay and home to Rawalpindi by train.

The boys continued to grow and enjoy their family life. They loved stories, and their mother read the stories of Rudyard Kipling's *Jungle Book* to them because the local setting was familiar to them. Even as little boys, they wanted more of Kipling, and so she read *Kim*, which opened with a boy playing on the cannons on display outside the government building in Lahore, just like the Maxwell boys had done. On a Sunday afternoon, Robert found his family enjoying *Kim*. He took exception to the reading of a secular book on the Sabbath and so began to teach his sons the Westminster Shorter Catechism. It became a great game to see who could get the right answers. As the boys grew older and more expert, even greater satisfaction came in correcting Father as he recited the questions.

Pollock and George continued to be active little boys. One day, their mother called to them repeatedly to stop jumping on the bed, until they came to her to claim that it was not they but tremors from an earthquake causing the rattling in the house. Two young boys growing up on the mission field, surrounded by talk of matters of faith, saw the hand of God in everything. One day, the boys were playing on the porch when they noticed the shadows cast by the lattice work were bending steadily, and the sky was growing darker. Convinced that the world was ending, they ran to find their mother, who explained the solar eclipse, to their amazement.

Teaching young boys the mysteries of the world, faith and etiquette were a daily focus. One day, when Pollock and George were walking with their father to a preaching post, each boy in turn felt the side of his father's boot gently applied to his bottom. Not missing a step, Robert got their attention and explained how he wanted them to politely greet the man who was walking down the road toward them.

The first order of business when the family arrived home from the States was floor covering. Robert sent for weavers, who cleared the house of furniture and wove matting from the front door to the back through every room in the house. The matting was covered with various rugs, but it made the floor relatively smooth and impervious to bugs (at least for a while).

Getting what was wanted was not always easy. Even before the

A Promised Life

matting was laid, Maud sent Robert to the market to find a new houseboy with instructions to bring back "anyone but Futtah." She had found it difficult to make him understand how she wanted things done before they went home. Robert returned with Futtah, explaining that no one else was available. No one else was ever available. The whole market knew that the Maxwells belonged to Futtah, and none of his cousins would apply for the job of houseboy. Futtah took great pride in his family.

Their house was located on the Great Trunk Road, with a brickwork up the road from the compound. It seemed to young Pollock and George that the donkeys would make good mounts when the straw baskets lashed to their sides were empty of bricks, and away they went to ride. They did not get far before Futtah snatched them off and informed them that his gentlemen did not stoop to riding donkeys.

Before that first year was out, the boys had outgrown the pajamas the family brought back from the States. Maud sent Futtah for the tailor and described what she wanted, but not well enough. Shortly, the flannel she provided was returned, sown into fine pajama tops with pants that fitted like riding jodhpurs because that is what the tailor had seen white gentlemen wear.

Natural life made for dangers, even in the house. Everyone always slept under netting to keep the mosquitoes and the malaria they carried at bay. Every house had a mongoose to sniff out and dispatch snakes. Even so, things were not always secure. Bathing at the Maxwell house was done in a tiled bathroom; one corner had a section where the tile sloped down to a corner with a drain that took used water out to water the roses. A dish of soap and water and an urn filled with clean rinse water stood by. One morning, Robert went in to bathe, having removed the glasses he wore to deal with his nearsightedness. When he had lathered up, he turned to reach for the urn. At that point, he noticed the urn was not its usual shape. The neck did not slope gracefully in and out but rather went straight up from the body. Squinting, he noticed a cobra coiled around the urn's neck, ready to strike. He froze in place for what must have seemed like hours until the snake got bored, uncoiled itself, and slithered through the drain pipe into the garden. At that point, Robert raised the cry of alarm; the mongoose and houseboy were dispatched to the garden to deal with the snake, which they did, and screen wire was added to the garden end of the drain to avoid future bath surprises.

In 1910, the family went through another year of change, as Pollock reached the age to go off to boarding school in the mountains. Because it was a special time, Pollock was asked what sort of cake he wanted for his birthday dinner. The request was coconut, his favorite. When cook finished the cake, she set it on the window ledge to cool until dinner. A monkey swung down and made off with the cake. In later years, that story produced many coconut birthday cakes for the boy who was deprived of one for his seventh birthday.

Shortly after his birthday, Pollock and his mother set off for Woodstock School, up in the foothills of the Himalayas in Landour, at about sixty-five hundred feet. American missionary children in the western part of north India, especially those of Presbyterian and Baptist churches, were educated there for generations, along with the children of British government officials. The cooler weather was considered healthier, and the Christian liberal arts education prepared the children well for later education at American and British colleges and universities.

Many of their parents first became acquainted with the school when they spent time in language school in Landour. Beginning in the first year, children were expected to study hard in a variety of subjects, including English grammar, French, Latin, German, mathematics, history, Bible, and the sciences. Woodstock had initially been a school for girls, dating back to 1854. It was purchased by the Presbyterian church for missionary children in 1872. The school had always enrolled Anglo Indians as well as British and American students. The school term was March through December. By the time the Maxwell family began attending, girls could board on campus; boys boarded either with their families or through private arrangements in a home near campus. Pollock set off with his mother and his trunk packed with school uniform and other essentials of life for a small boy. Today, it would be an eight-hour flight from Rawalpindi. For them, it was several days by train followed by a journey up into the mountains in a one axle ox cart, since the grade was too steep for a carriage.

At school, Pollock applied himself and worked to fit in. He

found more delight in soccer than in Latin, but he knew that he was expected to make his family proud and so studied hard. In addition to school courses, he learned the local dialect so he could communicate with local boys and shopkeepers. He also learned to knit, as he was expected to provide his own socks and needed thick ones as winter approached. He found that knickers and knees scraped on the soccer field did not mix well, and after a week of pulling off his scab daily, he had a decided limp. He had not found much tenderness from the faculty and staff at Woodstock up to this point and was rather missing his family. When the house mistress discovered the reason for his limp, a badly swollen and infected sore on the knee, she ordered him to bed and provided the comfort of nightly hot chocolate for a week until the sore had healed and he could return to class and fields. From then on, Pollock knew that there was kindness around him and felt at home in school.

When he arrived for his second year, his mother wanted to shop for some cloth before she left him. As they stood in the store, Pollock listened to the shopkeeper and his mother, who seemed to be having great trouble coming to terms. The shopkeeper was speaking the local dialect, but his mother addressed him in Urdu.

Finally, Maud rapped her son on the shoulder with her umbrella and said to him in English, "Tell that man what I want and ask him how much he wants for it."

In an instant, the boy clearly understood, to his astonishment, that not everyone knew all the languages he did. That year, he was called home early in November to meet his new brother, David. He was left alone with the baby when David started to fuss. Never having been left alone before with a baby in all his eight years, Pollock got down on his knees and prayed the good Lord to make his baby brother stop crying. During Pollock's fourth year at Woodstock, George joined him, and from then on, there was someone familiar always present at school, in addition to the crowd at home, who periodically sent letters and sometimes tins of Nabisco wafers.

***

While the next generation was growing and learning, Robert's role in the mission was expanding dramatically. When they returned from furlough, Robert was returned to the Boys' High School in Rawalpindi. In 1903, Rev. J. H. Morton had replaced Rev. W. B. Anderson as principal of Gordon College, when Dr. Anderson left to devote himself to district evangelistic work. In 1909, Rev. Morton went on furlough for a year. Dr. W. L. Porter had come from Yale to establish the science department and had done excellent work, making the department a leader among Indian schools to the point that by 1909, twenty of the twenty-three students who attempted the university science exams passed.

When Rev. Morton left, Dr. Porter was made acting principal of the college. Mrs. Porter had never recovered from the shock of the riots of 1907, and in 1909, they left for America. With Rev. Morton and Dr. Porter both gone, Robert, who had established a good reputation for himself as manager of the high school, was made acting principal of the college, as well. He knew most of the faculty from his days at the high school prior to furlough, but while the Maxwells had been in America, a new faculty member had come to join the college family. William H. Merriam came on a three-year appointment. He returned to the States in 1911 to marry, but the short-term assignment had worked so well that he brought his bride, Josephine, out in 1913 after a year in Princeton. They stayed in the field until long after the Maxwells came home. William Merriam and Robert Maxwell would work closely together first at the college and then as treasurer (William) and general-secretary (Robert) of the mission before William became first secretary treasurer of the mission, when those positions were combined. He also served as president of Gordon College.

By 1911, Robert's administrative duties as a minister had expanded substantially. He was on the Survey Committee of the mission, traveling to survey the best properties for building new schools and residences and to oversee construction that took place near Rawalpindi. He had been elected to a five-year term as translating clerk for the Sialkot Synod of the Presbyterian Church of North India. His work included translating the minutes of the synod meetings into English and forwarding them to the UPNA General Assembly so that the committee appointed by the General Assembly could know whether the missionaries were doing the work to they were appointed to do. He also was responsible for translating and editing Synod resolutions for church papers. The work of the mission had resulted in seven native presbyteries and the Sialkot Synod by this time, where the missionaries provided support and training (but leadership was work of the local clergy and elders). Robert's own work was made legible by the typewriter he had purchased from Dr. Porter years before. In 1911, he presided over the examination of two candidates for ordination in his presbytery in Urdu and was grateful that his language skills had grown to the point where that was possible. He wrote to his father to let him know all that he was doing, to thank him for his education, and to let him know that he was using every bit of the training he had received in his work. He was elected to a three-year term as clerk of the mission by his fellow missionaries but found these quarterly meetings, which were conducted in English, much less of a task than the translating work involved in his work for the Synod.

In 1914, his correspondence with the UPNA General Assembly Foreign Mission Office began to be filed at the request of his friend, Dr. W.B. Anderson, who wanted complete records of mission correspondence. Dr. Anderson left India that year to become corresponding secretary for foreign missions in the main office in Philadelphia.

This began a record of Robert's two-way correspondence with the board, which would last through the end of his mission service and is still on file at the Presbyterian Historical Society in Philadelphia. The synod elected him to the Publications Committee. When he began, he discovered that thirty-eight hundred of the five thousand copies of Persian-character Punjabi Psalms were still unsold. He led the missionaries in hustling themselves to get more of those texts into circulation. This was a part of the evangelistic work of the mission. Texts of the Psalms (and the Gospels later, as they were translated) were sold to any interested party on the streets and on the trains. When he was traveling by train with his father, Pollock was sent up and down the cars, offering copies of the Gospel of John for ten rupees.

With time to pass, many of the Indian passengers took advantage of the offer. Pollock was quite surprised when a Sikh tracked him down one trip to ask if he had more about this Jesus available. It was, he liked to say, his first conversion.

CHAPTER
7

Half a World Apart: 1915–1918

Changes came to the family again in 1915. Pollock had been severely ill, and the physicians Robert and Maud consulted finally concluded that he must return to America if he was to have any chance to live. The second part of Elizabeth's partnership would need to go into effect, that agreement that she would care for the children when they came to the States for their education. When the school year ended, Pollock was to sail with Margaret Wilson, who was going home for good after teaching for many years in the girls' school in Rawalpindi, where Maud taught. When the day came for Pollock to leave, Robert spoke to the family at breakfast before prayers. He instructed them that this would not be an easy parting, that he knew that the family would deeply miss Pollock's presence with them in India, that he was going home to preserve his health, and that if tears were to be shed, now in the family was the time for tears. Then he prayed for his son's safe passage and the return of his health. At the train station, young David, only four years old, burst into tears as it hit him that his biggest brother was leaving him. Robert was most embarrassed at young David's behavior. Pollock's clear memories of the journey home were of feeling secure with Aunt Margaret, whom he had known all his life, and the adventure of being a boy at sea. He was very impressed when the shooting stopped across the Suez Canal so that the ship could sail through in safety.

Pollock was sent out into a world at war. In June 1914, the archduke of Austria-Hungary, Ferdinand, was assassinated. In August, war was declared in Europe. Great Britain, France, and the Russian Empire were aligned against the central powers of Germany and Austria-Hungary. The war's end in 1918 triggered the collapse of the last modern empires of Russia, Germany, China, Ottoman Turkey, and Austria-Hungary. The Treaty of Versailles, the agreement by which the war was ended, required Germany to accept responsibility for causing all of the loss and damage of the war. Germany could not meet reparation requirements. They were renegotiated several times and indefinitely postponed in 1932. The treaty improved European relationships for a time, but it really satisfied no one and contributed to the rise of Nazism in Germany and to World War II. In Russia, the war led to the collapse of morale and economic chaos, which resulted in the Bolshevik Revolution in 1917 and Russian Civil War, which lasted until 1922 when Lenin's power was firmly established.

It was a time of social as well as political revolution. Many restaurants in Europe and the United States were equipped with dance floors. During this era, ballroom dancing was replaced more and more by jazz and the dances it inspired. In America, the partying and dancing were severely curtailed in 1919 with the ratification of the Eighteenth Amendment to the Constitution, which brought in Prohibition, which Charles and Elizabeth had pushed for. Hollywood replaced the East Coast as the center of the movie industry. In 1918, Warner Brothers Studios opened on Hollywood Boulevard. In the world of visual art, cubism, expressionism, and geometric abstractionism, which had been on the rise since the later nineteenth century, were joined by the Dada movement, which developed in reaction to the Great War, expressing nonsense, irrationality, and antibourgeois protest in visual, literary, and sound media. In 1916, the Summer Olympic Games were cancelled due to the war.

***

Things had changed in the field, not only due to the world conflict. In addition to his responsibilities at the American Mission High School in Gujranwala, where he had been assigned in 1911 to work as manager in partnership with a Mr. Chatterjee as principal, Robert was busy with larger mission business. He served on the executive committee of the Punjab Religious Book Society, was on the executive committee of the British and Foreign Bible Society, and chaired the committee to review the manual regulating governing relationships for the Board of Foreign Missions of the General Assembly of the UPCNA, as well as the Committee on Comity and Co-Operation in Intermission Activities. He was the clerk of the mission, responsible for minutes and communications with the General Assembly Office on Foreign Missions, and agreed when asked by the mission to extend his term as clerk through 1917 so that there would be stability in that office as the mission operations reorganized.

He served on the Municipal Council for the city of Gujranwala. He helped to organize the mission's Red Cross Committee to collect funds for the war wounded. His responsibilities for surveying sites for possible schools and housing continued to grow. As clerk of the mission, he had taken up regular correspondence with his good friend from the field, Dr. W. B. Anderson, with whom the Maxwells lived during their first six months in India. Dr. Anderson had left the field for work in the foreign mission office of the UPCNA General Assembly, and in June of 1916, he was made corresponding secretary for foreign missions for the assembly. Dr. Anderson asked Robert for reports on many things. In one letter, he asked him particularly to report on railway expansion locations and how those would affect the location of mission buildings. In another, he thanked him for the names and addresses of all the missionaries in the field, which was being published with twenty-five thousand copies being distributed in the church to replace the annual report. Robert noted in a letter to Elizabeth that there was so much to do that the danger was that nothing would be done and asked her prayers that he would do *something*.

In September 1916, while the family was in the hills at Murree Station, Miss Nannie J. Spenser was staying in the same house where the Maxwell family was on vacation. She was one of the early missionaries of the 1880s at Lyallpur, a city in the desert part of the Gujranwala Mission Station, and along with Miss Kate Hill, she established a school for girls. The two women claimed to have initiated Maud and Robert into mission service when they arrived in 1900. It was a lovely time of reunion and rest together, but on September 5, Miss Spenser was stricken in the night with malaria and died. Robert reflected to Elizabeth that she was a person of excellent judgment who carried out many responsibilities. He remembered her saying that if a person waited long enough at mission meetings, someone wise would say what needed to be said. Her death was one of many sudden losses of dear friends and colleagues in the field.

Fortunately, the news from home indicated that Pollock was recovering his health. Robert wrote to say that he hoped that he would get the malaria out of his system and show signs of life. He asked Charlie to be sure Pollock got plenty of exercise. By October, he was doing pretty well and helping with the potato harvest. Robert was glad to know he had been put to work since "boys from India have to learn to use their own hands." He asked Elizabeth to ask Pollock to memorize 1 Corinthians 16:13–14: "Keep alert, stand firm in your faith, be courageous, be strong. Let all that you do be done in love."

He observed that at Murree, they were eating many good things including beans, peas, tomatoes, and corn, though he was sure the bill of fare in Gujranwala would be more limited. Disease was a constant threat on both continents. Elizabeth wrote of whooping cough in the community and an outbreak of polio in New York State. Robert wrote of plague, which had reached Rawalpindi but not yet Gujranwala in India. Pollock still had a cough, and his father requested that Elizabeth be sure he sleep with the windows open.

By October, the family was down from the hills and again settled in Gujranwala, having arrived by motorcar. Dr. John McConnelee had had the first Ford auto in the field, which arrived some years before. The car was shared by everyone, who quickly learned the tricks to keep it going. As the family traveled from Murree, the car stalled. The driver had worked on it for some time with no success when Maud fished a hairpin out of her hair and dug out the clog in the carburetor, which got it going again.

India was directly involved in the war as a part of the British Empire. Robert reflected that the Republicans had misjudged President Wilson's strength in America, and he trusted that the president would be guided to do right in the crisis before him. He was glad for the president's patience in the conflict, and he was very glad that his calm and wise former teacher was head of his country's government in the unstable days of wartime.

The war had several immediate effects on the mission. Students and faculty members volunteered or were conscripted to serve. Chatterjee observed to those graduating that the fifty or sixty rupees they would be granted as soldiers, along with meals and uniforms, would be more than they would be likely to receive in any other employment available to them. Eleven or twelve of the eighteen graduates that year who joined the military were Christians. Funds for the mission were limited due to the anxiety about the war and the global economic impact it was having. Robert wrote to Anderson that the news was sufficiently startling, but they were not as badly off as some others. The Lutheran mission was cut by ten thousand pounds sterling. He said he believed that Anderson had "hold of the true situation, we have to rely on the loving kindness of our God." The newspapers were calling for the government to forbid German missionaries in India, and other missions, especially the Anglicans, were attempting to minister to those converts with no mission support after the Germans left.

There was much anxiety among the Presbyterians in the States about their missionaries in the field. Robert wrote to Anderson that he felt safer than he had in the riots of 1907, and that sentiment seemed to be shared among all the missionaries in the Sialkot mission. He reported that he was of the opinion that they would not be in danger unless the Germans were much more successful; instead, he felt that the Germans would rapidly decline. Anderson was much relieved with this report, and without naming the source, he wrote in an article for the newspaper that he had received assurance from a trusted missionary that their mission field in India was quiet. He observed that having Indian troops in so many parts of the world during the war would make a difference in India afterwards, in openness to different ideas and to faith in Christ.

Social upheaval on the subcontinent of India became more clearly pronounced in 1916. The government issued a decree that aliens would no longer be permitted to serve on municipal councils or other areas of government. Robert was delighted to be relieved of the tedium of municipal council meetings and resigned. Of more serious concern to missions was the government's call for freedom in schools from the requirement that students be required to receive religious instruction. According to a manual adopted in August, all schools and colleges in India that received government funds were required to develop a conscience clause. The manual contained the following statement regarding the missions of the Punjab and the guiding principles for their schools:

> There are only three references to religion in the Educational Code of the Punjab
>
> (Article 36) Grants-in-aid are given only for secular instruction and without reference to any religious instruction.
>
> (Article 46) the following are the conditions on which maintenance grants are given...
>
> (k)that the school in all its departments is open to inspection as laid down by Article 39, provided that it shall be no part of the duty of any one inspecting an aided school to examine any pupil or to enquire into any instruction given in religious knowledge.
>
> (Article 240) Religious instruction shall not be given in Government or Board Schools except out of school hours, and then only at the express request of the parents concerned. No teacher employed in a Government or Board school shall be required to give such instruction without his consent, and no charge on account of religious instruction shall be paid from public funds.
>
> From the above extracts from the Punjab Educational Code it will be seen that the Punjab leaves all aided schools free as to what arrangements they shall

make in regard to religious education, and to the best of my knowledge so long as the secular teaching is in accordance with the scheme laid down by the department, in no case whether a single area school or not, does the department interfere in the question of religious teaching at all. It is teachers in Government and Board schools who may, at the express request of the parents, teach boys religion outside of school hours. R. Force Jones[28]

Robert was a member of the Executive Committee of Punjab Representative Council of Christian Mission and its representative to the National Missionary Council, the group responsible for negotiating with the government on how missions would carry out the conscience clause provisions and other matters related to government and mission relationships. In 1917, the National Missionary Council met with government officials. Robert and the bishop of Nagpur were entertained at the palace, and he rode the train from Lucknow with committee members and high officials of other denominations. The missionaries found the government had already acted to discontinue lotteries for military service (they were exempt from compulsory military service). The government leaders were willing at that point to continue funding for schools that made religious instruction voluntary and not paid for with public funds.

The policies for complying with government standards for religious education was a taxing matter in the negotiations among the missionaries. The second area of negotiations was maybe even more stressful. Under Dr. Anderson's leadership, the General Assembly was developing its own manual governing the denomination's relationships with missions. This manual was the cause of much detailed correspondence between two longtime friends, correspondence that could have become quite hostile had they not been such good friends. When the draft manual was sent for mission review, Robert made copies available to all the missionaries and appointed a committee to work with him to compile a response, including questions and suggestions to offer back to the foreign mission board. In the response, Robert wrote strongly in favor of equal pay for male and female single missionaries, arguing that if the members of the board could see the conditions in which female missionaries lived on their salaries, they would not be allowed to continue. He also argued for half-salary for missionaries on furlough instead of the very small stipend allotted. He made a strong case for encouraging women who went out for a year as associate missionaries to stay longer, even if they didn't wish to become permanent missionaries, as their language skills and their knowledge of the work made them invaluable. He made a case that the mission should be heard before a decision was made on whether to continue the appointment of a missionary at the end of first term, since the mission knew the person's usefulness better than the board could know at a distance. The review committee requested that taxes levied by the British on missionary income be paid not out of salary but by the board. Of course, the missionaries paid US income taxes, but Robert argued that they would not be in British India at all if the board had not sent them there. He raised issue with the language about a property purchase, noting that when someone has agreed to sell, the time it took to consult with the board and get a decision would usually be unworkable and unfair to the seller and would make it impossible to procure property for which there was a demand on the market. To each of these points, Anderson replied with thanks and the understanding of a former missionary in the field. He noted that with all his work in drafting the manual, he had not seen how the language could raise the concerns Robert and the committee had raised. He was grateful and would make adjustments for clarity so that when the matter went to the General Assembly, the product would be policies both the missionaries and the board could understand and live with.

Robert shared with Anderson his frustration that his work on behalf of the mission continued to take time away from his primary work with the school. He wrote that he had not begun work on a boarding house. He hoped that after the mission's annual meeting in the spring of 1917, he would be free from official and committee work and able to devote himself to the school and the building. He reported that there was division in schools, both in Rawalpindi and in Gujranwala, over boarding houses. Chatterjee echoed the feeling of many families that there should be a separate school for Christian boys. Some felt that non-Christian teachers did not give fair attention to Christian students. Robert disagreed but felt that none of the boys got enough individual attention for their education. He regretted that he hadn't been able to give them enough of his time, that there was no short-term teacher able for tutoring in the Christian faith, and that there were non-Christian teachers. He believed that a separate hostel for the Christian students, which had not been tried in the mission, could have a good effect.

The idea of a Christian high school for boys was popular among mission personnel and educated and high caste people. This possibility surfaced the year before at the Sialkot mission meeting and continued to be popular. A committee was established to give advice on how to proceed. Two members visited Tuskegee and Hampton, both Presbyterian boarding schools in America, before coming out to India. It was surprising to Robert that Chatterjee, who had devoted his life to educating Christian and non-Christian alike, had expressed the idea that teaching non-Christians in mission schools had about run its course. He noted to Anderson that the boys read their Bibles and loved and respected Chatterjee, but they did not come out openly and confess Christ.

The other area of great concern to him at this time was the more general question of evangelistic work. Native pastors were assigned to evangelistic work, but health issues and the concern of wives in moving far from other Christians made the assignments to new areas slow going. Mission doctors treated cholera, malaria, and typhoid and prescribed nourishing diets; the pastors seemed to be improving physically, so Robert was hopeful that the work could soon be expanded, as they developed stamina for it.

***

Family life was never far from Robert's mind and Maud's, even if their eldest child was half a world away. Elizabeth was faithful to report on Pollock's health and habits, even as she shared word of her own contributions to the war efforts, working with the Red Cross and helping with the census. Those letters were an important connection, but the war made mail unreliable and slow in coming, at best. On

August 9, 1917, Robert wrote to Pollock to tell him how glad he was that Pollock had joined the church at age fourteen. He counseled him to remember that he had given himself to God and agreed to be his boy every day and all day and to trust God to help in everything he wanted Pollock to do. Maud wrote to tell him that after his two-year absence, young David talked about his oldest brother when no one else had mentioned him, showing that even the youngest among them felt Pollock's absence and missed him.

They tried to keep him up on family news, Robert writing proudly in one letter that Pollock's mother had taken first place in her course in first aid. He reflected that when Pollock left them, they didn't know that the war would extend to America by mid-1917 and that as American troops were training to join the fight in France, Robert hoped they would help to bring the war to a speedy end. Robert asked his son to pray for God's guidance not only for himself but also for his family in India and for his friends. What they did not tell him, but was of great concern to them, was that his brothers were suffering from illness, much as he had done. Wallace had missed a year of school due to illness. While his health was the greatest concern, George and David were ill far too often for his anxious parents, who had already lost one child and had known the loss of several friends and their children.

Robert and Maud eagerly anticipated the year of 1918, when they would sail for America and a second furlough home, with stops across the country to share the story of their work and time to visit family in Pittsburgh and Cambridge. They would have to decide whether it was time for all four boys to move to the States to complete their education. Wally and David each had a pet chicken. Two weeks before the family was to leave for America, Wally's chicken went missing, and chicken was served for lunch. That afternoon, David gave his chicken to a native family who lived on the compound so that it would not meet the fate of its sister chicken. It did not end up in anybody's dinner pot (at least until the family had gone).

The family traveled from Calcutta to San Francisco on the SS *Santa Cruz*. The *Santa Cruz* was a large ship built in 1913 to carry passengers and freight between the Port of San Francisco and the Asian markets. This trip took Robert, Maud, and the boys through a part of the world they had not seen before. It was quite an adventure for everyone. George (age twelve), Robert (nine), and young David (six) could play at being pirates when they were not taking in the sights of places they had only heard about. They sailed east past Malaysia, Australia, New Guinea, and Hawaii, with stops along the way until they came to the vast Pacific Ocean and saw no land at all, until they sighted the coast of California. They set sail on May 16, 1918, and arrived in San Francisco on July 4, just in time for the celebration of Independence Day. The day after they landed, Maud wrote to Pollock from the Hotel Ramona on hotel stationery, with a colored picture of a native American girl and a group of braves. She longed to see him right away, but first there were trips, to Kansas City for a week and then to Pittsburgh to see the Pollocks there. Her brother, Robert, was still in France with the US Army. She had had no word from him lately and was eager to get to her mother and learn what she knew about how he was. The war would end in November, and he would come home to Pittsburgh, but she could not know that yet.

The boy who greeted them in Cambridge was in many ways different from the boy who left home three years before. His grandfather, George S. Maxwell, died in June of 1915 just as Pollock arrived for his own recuperation. The farm passed to Charlie, now grown and married to Alice Arnott, with four children of his own. Pollock was an admired older cousin to Charles's children, and the fact that three of the four were near the ages of his own younger brothers must have eased the pain of separation from his family. Mary, the cousin who was Wallace's age, would remember all her life the beautiful blue eyes of her cousin Pollock and how kind he was to her and to her sisters and brother.

School had been a shock. Years later, Pollock, by then known to all as Bill, would say that in many ways, his love of learning faded that first day in the one-room school, when the boy reading aloud beside him read about a lead statue and pronounced the word *lead* not like what pipes were made of but like what you do with a bridled horse. A boy who had read in three languages when he was seven was sure that this school had nothing further to teach him, and so he made no effort to learn and only marginal effort to keep up with assignments.

By the time his parents arrived in 1918, he was rising from bed each morning before daylight to milk the family cows before he left for school. He returned home to complete the other chores his uncle had for him, but he was less than compliant. Boys from India learned independence early because they were away from family in school for much of the time. This was all foreign to Charles's life experience, and the two clashed frequently. At the age of fifteen, Pollock was planning to leave school and sharecrop until he could afford a farm of his own. There was a girl he liked, and farming seemed like something he could do well. He even was able to yoke the draft horses without a struggle. He had figured out that if he yoked them so that the one who was blind in one eye could not see the other, they did fine.

When they arrived in New York, Robert and Maud found a headstrong boy with clear ideas of his own. After Charlie told his brother he ought to discipline his son and see if he could teach him some respect for his elders, Robert and Pollock retired to the woodshed. After some time of Robert applying his belt to his boy, he paused, and Pollock asked his father if he had had enough. His father applied himself with renewed vigor for a time, and then Pollock explained that Charlie chased him with a pitchfork or beat him severely when he was angry. A belt was a pretty tame means of discipline by comparison.

He also shared his plans with his father, and Robert was quick to inform him that what he ultimately did with his life was his business, but his father expected him to complete his education, including college, first. Apparently, his parents talked over with each other the situation with regard to their four sons and decided that the best plan was for Maud to remain in America with them. Robert would rent a house for the family, and Pollock and George would attend the high school in Cambridge. Robert wrote to Anderson in October to inquire about short-term furlough so that he could move his family to a college town when the time came. Anderson replied that the board had a policy offering a short furlough after four years when a missionary's wife remained in America with the children. He was glad to lay this before the board as a request from Robert. Furlough pay was ninety dollars per month, and the short mid-term furlough was allowed because there was only the expense of one person traveling.

And so it came to be that at the end of furlough in 1918, the family was again separated, this time with one member in India and five in America. In Cambridge, Maud developed the habit of telling her sons goodbye at the door whenever they were going out with the words, "Remember that you are a Maxwell and make us proud."

CHAPTER
8

Cambridge and Gujranwala: 1918–1922

Life in Cambridge was a new experience for the five Maxwells there. Upstate New York on the Vermont border offered a radically different climate than they had known. What people there called mountains were nothing to the Himalayas, where they had spent school terms, and where they were used to escaping the searing summer heat on the plains of the Punjab. Anyone familiar with Grandma Moses' paintings knows what the rolling hills of Washington County, New York, look like. In winter, they were excellent for sledding and skiing. In late summer, they were a green backdrop to golden fields of hay, rye, and corn.

The rhythms of life were different too. February brought syrup making, as maple trees were tapped and sap boiled down in open vats for syrup finished on farm stoves. October brought apple butter making, again in large outdoor vats, stirred all night by everyone, adult and child, in turn. Christmas time, people decorated their homes with sweet-smelling evergreen branches. As Thanksgiving drew near, the boys helped Aunt Elizabeth tend her turkeys on weekends. Barn raisings and horseshoeing were times for the community to gather, and of course so was church on Sundays.

These were not gatherings like they had known back in India of missionary friends, who shared meals most days. Here, farm people worked from sunup to sundown, and they ate with their families unless there was a special occasion. Cattle were reddish brown or white and black, not the long-horn Brahmas of India, and they were valued for their usefulness, not treated as sacred. Farmwork, including plowing and harvesting, was done with sturdy horses called Morgans, useful for both work and riding. In India, mules passed their homes burdened with goods for market or building supplies. Horses were used by the British officers. Plowing and planting and harvesting were done by men with help from animals and sophisticated machinery like the threshing machines, which the boys loved to watch in the fields.

Money was very tight. Maud baked bread to sell and sold eggs from the family chickens, with David and Wallace making deliveries in town with their Red Flyer wagon. Much of the time, the weather was so cold and dry that her fingers cracked and bled. Pollock learned to knead the dough to spare his mother's fingers. Maud took in laundry, and Pollock, who had a reputation as a good worker, continued to work on neighboring farms during planting and harvest seasons; he also assisted the local undertaker. George helped his mother as well, but he was far more dedicated to his studies than his elder brother. The boys found American school much less demanding than in India. Pollock found more challenge in the several classes each day in high school than he had in the one-room country school near the farm. Maud was glad to take on the responsibility for dealing with bills and orders for Robert, now that she was back in the States. They both recognized the great work Elizabeth had done for them, but having lived in India, Maud was sure she would know best just what Robert needed for the school and for himself.

November of 1918 brought the end of the war, and the soldiers began to return. Maud and Robert were delighted to hear from her mother (and from her brother, Robert, himself) of his safe return. Many men returned weakened and sick from their time away. They had lived too much of the war in open trenches in mud. Trench fever, typhoid, malaria, influenza, and pneumonia were constant dangers; many men came home weakened as a result of these illnesses and the constant lack of adequate food. As had been true for Pollock and for his grandfather when he returned from the Civil War, the healthy rural climate of Washington County had a healing effect on those returning there. Other disabilities from the war, limbs lost to mortars or machine guns, lungs permanently scarred by poison gas, could not be healed. The advanced weapons of this war produced millions of casualties worldwide in four short years.

With less responsibility for her brother's family, Elizabeth was able to be more active in support of her congregation and its general mission work. She helped her sister-in-law, Alice, as they continued her mother's habit of hosting visiting preachers and family in their home. She continued to be active in the temperance movement, and in 1920, she voted in an election for the first time, after the Nineteenth Amendment was ratified that year. Both Susan B. Anthony and Elizabeth Cady Stanton, the early leaders of the suffrage movement, were native New Yorkers. Stanton grew up just west of Washington County in Johnstown. In 1878, they had been instrumental in getting Congress to consider a constitutional amendment granting voting rights for women (the amendment ultimately was ratified in 1920). Elizabeth had kept up with the suffrage movement all her life.

She was again the family correspondent. Cousins wrote from as far away as Indiana and Kansas to share family news. She corresponded with people she knew through the church, as well. In 1919, she received a formal request for the loan of the minutes of the UPNA General Assembly from the Board of Home Mission in Pittsburgh. The board's copy was incomplete, and they had learned that Elizabeth held the minutes her uncle, George Telford, had kept until his death. The request mentioned that if she would like to give them to the board, they would be a welcome gift. A second letter from the board thanking Elizabeth for the loan suggests that Miss Maxwell was of the opinion that if she had the only complete set, she better hold on to it.

Christmas time in 1920 brought a letter from Mrs. Blanche Anderson, wife of Robert's good friend and colleague, Dr. W. B. Anderson, corresponding secretary for foreign mission. Mrs. Anderson thanked Libbie for her hospitality when the Andersons visited the presbytery and sent her best wishes for Christmas and the New Year.

***

In 1919, Robert returned alone from New York to Gujranwala, taking the European route, which was much less exciting now that the war had ended. He was assigned to the Christian Training Institute in Sialkot, where he was glad to have a hand in preparing young Christian men for their practical work, supporting their families, and their evangelistic work, contributing to the growing Christian witness in their country.

In February of 1920, he was selected by the synod to serve on the executive committee of the New World Movement of the Synod. The Protestant New World Movement was a global program of evangelistic outreach. It was created to coordinate worldwide efforts among denominations to share Christ's love with those who had not known it. The promoters of the movement felt that this united effort worldwide would provide for stronger Christian witness, as both foreign and domestic evangelists could learn from each other across denominational lines. Robert felt that it could have a very positive influence on public opinion toward mission in the United States and was glad to serve. The committee was made up of four leaders of the church in India and three missionaries. In addition, it had a missionary and a native representative from the Women's Missionary Society of the synod. Because of his previous survey work for the mission, Robert was elected to serve as head of survey work.

His work for the mission as part of the team to acquire property and build buildings needed for schools, hospitals, and housing for students and missionaries meant that he was now asked to provide the Philadelphia office with copies of all deeds and drawings of the dimensions of the buildings. The other missionaries with whom he had done this work in years past were back in the States by this time, and so the work was his to do.

Thus began a season of ministry in which Robert divided his time between the mission office in Sialkot and the schools in Sialkot and in Gujranwala, where he had been before furlough. He shared housing with missionary friends in both places. He devoted his time to administrative work and the strengthening of the mission in practical ways, looking for funding and for property so that the work could expand. It was a season with a particular emphasis on administrative work, as in both the government offices in India and the halls of the foreign mission office in Philadelphia, there was a call for documentation and accountability more than ever. As the constitution for the mission was being ratified to be approved by the board at home, he argued that the women missionaries needed full voting rights, especially the single women, who were there on their own call, not as part of a family unit. At a time when the government of the United States had given women the right to vote, could the mission do less? Even in the midst of administration, his concern was ever the welfare of the missionaries and of the church they served.

He commented in his letters to Dr. Anderson that he did not have much time to miss his family in America. In one of those letters, he asked about Dr. Anderson's daughter, Leila, who had surgery the summer before she was to start college. He was glad to learn that she was well enough to begin school in the fall term at Westminster College in New Wilmington. He asked for Dr. Anderson's thoughts on possible schools for his own children, noting that he was partial to Princeton, but that the snobbery there could be a negative influence on his sons. Maud was very concerned about having to look after four teenaged boys, with their father half the world away, and feared they might stray from the right path. Robert wrote to her to assure her that only God could save the boys from that, and he was confident that God would. He knew he could not save them. Dr. Anderson sympathized with Robert's concern for his sons' education and for funding the cost. He said that Westminster was having some internal problems just then but was confident those would get sorted before the Maxwell boys were ready for college and added that Muskingum was enjoying a really good reputation for the quality of its educational and spiritual programs.

Robert was very disappointed with America's failure to support the League of Nations, after President Wilson had gotten the international community to agree to at the time of the Paris peace accord ending the war. President Wilson suffered a crippling stroke in 1919 and died in 1920. The league had been supported most strongly by the president, and he was not willing to compromise with the Senate leadership on the particulars of the plan for the league, nor did he take any of the leaders with him to Paris. Following his death, President Warren Harding took office, pledging to oppose the league, and the Senate shortly voted to refuse to participate. It would take another world war and a new generation of national leaders to see the wisdom of an international forum to promote understanding and justice among nations, leading to the United Nations, based on the vision of the league. Robert was concerned about the Bolshevik revolt in Russia and the implications there might be for widespread socialist uprisings in Asia. Robert did not think the Bolsheviks would have much direct influence in India, but he was concerned about the ongoing frontier war with Afghanistan.

The political situation in India following the war had its own dramatic turns, not unrelated to the rest of the world. Many Muslim Indians in these years were selling their property cheap and emigrating to Afghanistan. While this made for great opportunities to purchase property for mission expansion, it was difficult to see people leave because they had been told they could not live in India and be good Muslims. The Defense of India Act of 1915 had been passed to curtail nationalistic and revolutionary activities during and after the war. It applied to any British subject but was used overwhelmingly against Indians to curtail any genuine political dialogue. This made it hugely unpopular with all Indian people and was a major reason the members of the Muslim community were leaving.

In 1921, in the midst of negotiating for property for the new mission hospital in Taxila, the deputy secretary in charge of negotiating with the mission had a health breakdown and left for England, following the massacre of eighty-six members of the Sikh community at Nankana. The Sikhs showed tremendous restraint in refusing to retaliate against the corrupt town leaders who had sanctioned the slaughter. They were given self-rule of their area by the British government and won the praises of Mahatma Gandhi for adding to the prestige and glory of India. One letter Robert sent to Dr. Anderson in 1920 contained a clipping about a rail workers' strike for better wages in the northwest of India.

In the midst of political and social unrest around them, the work of the mission went on. Early in 1920, Robert sent a statistical report for the mission schools and the hospitals in the region. These included four high schools, a middle school in Martinpur, a girls' middle school in Rawalpindi, a girls' boarding school and city school, both in Sialkot, the Boys' Industrial Home and the Christian Training School, both in Gujranwala, Gordon College in Rawalpindi, and the seminary in Sialkot. There were hospitals in Jhelum, Pasrur, Sargodha, Bhera, and Sialkot and a home for women in Gundaspur. He noted that the seminary had graduated eighty-three and the business school six that year. In the south of India, missionaries had given up practical skills training for a more classic general liberal arts curriculum.

The Indian government's increasingly specific requirements for practical training made it almost impossible for mission schools, who could not afford to buy the large tracts of land required to teach agriculture or hire the additional staff required to teach the variety of electives specified. The government offered the Boys' Industrial Home equipment and staff to provide a two-year course in telegraph work. It would require a minimum of eight boys to take the course. Robert hoped they would take advantage of the opportunity. He wrote to consult with Dr. Anderson on using funds allocated by the board for the Christian Training School for the Boys' Industrial Home instead. The Christian Training School had other funds available, since it was newer, and the industrial home provided the practical training so many of the boys really needed to prepare them for skilled labor to support themselves. The mission hoped to strengthen it to become a high school as soon as possible. He heard talk of closing the high school in Sialkot to save money, so school funding was much on his mind.

During the summer months in Landour, Robert shared rooms with an English missionary, Dr. Bandy, and enjoyed very much hearing about his experience in the south of India. Dr. Bandy told him that schools in the south were closing, and the missionaries concentrated on helping the people better their lives. He had some very practical ideas for that work, including freezing hides of dead animals until better prices could be gotten for them in the months when fewer animals died, buying land when it was cheap on the market so that Indian Christians could farm it, and encouraging boys to collect pig bristles to sell for brushes. Robert agreed strongly with him that practical work as well as spiritual work were part of evangelism.

The government's interest in education was a very positive thing for the long-term welfare of the Indian people and their society. It was a challenge to negotiate for the missions. In 1921, Robert was on the board of Kinard College for Women in Lahore, which was faced with closing. The government had plans to open its own college for women in Lahore; Kinard College prepared women for professions, including especially medical professions. The missionaries feared there would not be enough college women to support two colleges. The government wanted higher education for women, without exposure to the Christian religion.

Dr. Anderson wrote to ask for an accounting of what was needed to bring Kinard up to a standard that would make it an acceptable college to the government so that he could work with the board in Philadelphia to raise the necessary funds. He noted that the church could no longer afford to be provincial but must work with the indigenous leaders if anything was to get done. He asked Robert to find a young, energetic missionary with fresh eyes to write articles for the church papers back home to detail the important work the Boys' Industrial Home was doing and to help raise support for the education of girls.

The missionaries had their internal difficulties with their schools. Robert was appointed to the seminary board, he believed, because the other missionaries on the board "did not feel up to standing up to the faculty" in the matter of the exams for ordination and saw Robert, he thought, as one "who shrank from no opportunity to assert himself." [29]

He wrote to Anderson that the chair of the board, Rev. Vazir Chad, had grown more than any man Robert knew since the days when he was in Robert's Bible class in Rawalpindi in 1901. Robert asked for prayers for the seminary, where Dr. Scott had been asked to resign as head over tensions with the faculty. While Dr. Scott had been distracted with the building program in Lahore, Dr. McConnelee was distracted with the work of the general treasurer of the mission, and Rev. Labhu, another faculty member, had been distracted by arguments with his wife and her family. The Women's Christian Medical College in Ludhiana was supported by several denominations' missions. The director, Dr. E. M. Brown, was asked to resign because of theological differences among the missions. Dr. Brown was seen as far too liberal by one element. In that matter, a legal opinion was sought, and the college was allowed to fall into what Robert saw as a disgusting state. The seminary, the leadership of the mission schools, and the church in India as a whole needed spiritual development if they were to be strong in Christian witness.

In the spring of 1921, Robert was able to send the deeds and drawings of buildings to the office in Philadelphia. It had not been a simple task. He employed two draftsmen to produce accurate scale drawings of the buildings so there would be a clear picture of exactly what the church owned. When there was need for expansion later, these drawings would provide evidence of why space was no longer adequate. The drawings were a huge task, since the mission owned considerable property, and no drawings had been done in the whole history of the mission, dating back to 1854.

Producing the deeds was, if anything, more difficult. Some were on hand in the synod office files, but more were missing. Some had been destroyed in government office fires. When the mission could produce its copies of original deeds, the government graciously registered them at no cost to the mission. The deed to the seminary was in a safe in Dr. McConnelee's house and had been eaten by ants. It was being recreated de novo again at no cost to the mission, since the government copy was destroyed by fire. Robert was greatly helped in locating and preparing the deeds needed by Mrs. Miller and three young women teachers. He was very glad to be finished with the task after sending seventy-one certified deeds to America in the capable hands of Dr. McConnelee. That same spring, Robert was made secretary of the mission and continued as its representative to the New World Movement Committee for 1921–1922.

The survey of possible sites to expand the mission and negotiating for property for those new locations took up a good deal of Robert's time. The fact that each expenditure needed the approval of the foreign mission board made it almost impossible to negotiate for an existing house for a missionary family; by the time approval came, the house would be sold to someone else. Until roads and rail lines were definitely plotted, it was difficult to know what property would be desirable for hospitals or schools by its proximity to transportation. For the former problem, Dr. Anderson suggested a list of proposed sites with cost estimates attached so that the board could do a general approval and speed the process with money to be expended as property was located.

Housing for missionaries was a constant concern. Robert was particularly concerned for the women, who served at such low pay and seemed to have the least privacy, as they lived in boarding houses, sharing rooms with other women near the schools where they taught or the hospitals where they worked. For families going to new mission stations, he felt keenly the need to get them out of tents and into permanent housing, whether preexisting and purchased or new built, before the rains came each year. Now that the missionaries were using Landour for summer retreats after the earthquake destroyed the housing in Dharmsala, he saw the need for four additional bungalows. By the end of 1921, Robert was in negotiations for two additional sites in new towns to expand the mission's work, with several more possible sites.

One major piece of real estate that consumed much of his time was the location and acreage for the new frontier hospital. The mission agreed that the hospital needed to be located north of the Jhelum River, but there was a lot of territory between the Jhelum and the Afghan border. After many trips to survey a wide variety of sites, along with Dr. E. L Porter of Gordon College, Dr. Martin, who would be the physician responsible for the new hospital, and others from the mission, it was finally decided that Taxila was the right location.

Somehow, Taxila must have seemed particularly appropriate in terms of its association with the Christian faith in India. Tradition had it that the apostle Thomas traveled as far as Taxila in the first century, and now, in the midst of a predominately Muslim tribal people, the Gospel would be back in the form of a Christian hospital in a small town in a remote area, twenty miles north of Rawalpindi. The Grand Trunk Road, the main road from Lahore up through the Khyber Pass into Afghanistan, passed through Taxila, and there was to be a major rail station there, as well.

Dr. Porter purchased fifty acres of land for the hospital without mission approval, but it proved to be a fine location for the hospital, which is still in operation there to this day. On June 8, 1921, Robert sent off his annual letter to Dr. Anderson for the board, detailing the building and equipment needs for the hospital and housing compound needs for staff. He also requested the board's permission to buy land for a school and for a house for Dr. Clements and his family in Badomali, the next location for mission expansion; he noted that the money contributed for missionary housing through the New World Movement would be spent as soon as decisions could be made on sites. The mission had to get in line behind the civil authorities in purchasing desirable property.

In August, he sent a follow-up letter detailing changes to the plans for the Taxila hospital. There was to be a dispensary, open whenever the hospital was open, an administration building and operating block, and two ward buildings, with two more to be added later to form a square when there was sufficient money from patients. Each block was to have three family rooms for family members staying with the patient. In addition, there would be a cook house, the house surgeon's house, nurses' quarters, servants' quarters, cooking sheds and latrines, a mortuary, a chapel, and at a later date, a maternity ward. Total cost for the land and buildings was proposed to be $88,154. Dr. Anderson replied following the board's meeting to thank Robert for his good report and to share the news that the board had released twenty thousand dollars to begin the building.

The work was not all administration. There was also pastoral care for those missionaries who were ill, whether the ailments were physical or due to the emotional stress of working in a region where conflict and violence were too near at hand, and daily life was foreign to those new to the field. Robert asked the board to send missionaries out earlier in the year so that they could become acquainted with mission life before they went off to language school. The six months he and Maud had spent in Rawalpindi before school in Landour had been very important in their own sense of belonging to the mission community years before. That community was a great source of comfort and support and fun in mission life.

When the synod met at Gujranwala in April 1921, he felt that strong sense of community support. He noted in a letter to Dr. Anderson that the young women teachers in Gujranwala had led the whole group in showing extraordinary ingenuity. He treasured opportunities to worship with the Punjabi Christians. In 1920, he spent a month of Sundays with the 71st Punjabi Regiment while Dr.

Stewart, their regular chaplain, took vacation. They and others at the mission were working to keep the regiment together, both for the welfare of the men who, he believed, benefitted from the order of military life and for the security of the Christian community in a region where religious differences sometimes resulted in riots and violence against those of other faiths, whether Sikh, Hindu, Islam, or Christian.

In addition to conducting formal religious services, he spent time with soldiers in conversation and visited those in hospital. Several were hospitalized for treatment of venereal disease. Robert observed in a letter to Dr. Anderson that "a regiment is a hard place to be just what you should be." He was glad that the mission could provide spiritual comfort and support to the soldiers. During the war, it had been served by a native chaplain educated at the mission seminary, and now Dr. Stewart served as chaplain. The regiment provided stability for the region and gave its members a chance to live together in a close interfaith community, where they learned respect for each other beyond their differences as they worked together to protect each other as well as those they served.

At times, the distance and the concern about providing for the education of their boys must have seemed overwhelming, especially for Maud. She and Robert wrote to each other regularly, and as the years passed until Robert's midterm furlough, when the family would move for college years, a plan emerged. It was the beginning of the 1920s, a postwar economic boom was driving up prices, including college tuition prices. In East Coast cities especially, a new lifestyle was emerging. Women were raising their skirts and bobbing their hair. Jazz had taken over the clubs and sometimes, it seemed, the radio waves, as well.

Maud was lonely in Washington County. She was surrounded by family, but it was Robert's family, and their ways were not her ways. For all those reasons, western Pennsylvania seemed more attractive as a place for the boys to attend college. In 1916, Charles Wallace, a cousin, was appointed president of Westminster. He was reported to be doing great things to deal with the issues that had concerned Dr. Anderson. Westminster was where Robert spent his first year of college. It was a UPNA school, and New Wilmington was a popular retirement place for missionaries. It likely never occurred to them to consult their children about their preference for college. They developed a plan to educate their boys in a place where they would be surrounded by good Christians and friends from the mission field and near enough to the Pollocks for regular visits. And so, in addition to his work in the field, Robert spent much of 1922 making plans to move his family once again when he came home.

CHAPTER

9

New Wilmington and Taxila: 1923–1928

Robert came to New York to move his family west to New Wilmington. There are no records of the exact time of his travel, but it must have been late 1922 or early 1923, since he returned to India in September 1923, once the family was established and the boys in school. This furlough brought limited time for visits with congregations and people interested in Robert's work. He and Elizabeth stayed in touch, of course. She forwarded to him a letter from their cousin, Anna Rawles, in Kansas City. Robert had written to her from the ship on the way home, but after the move, Anna did not know where to write to him. Elizabeth had the offer of a communion set for India, and while thanking her for the offer, Robert noted that the church in India usually did not use individual cups, but he would gladly take the gift and find a congregation that could use it. He was glad to hear of a summer convention held at Round Lake near Saratoga, New York, and hoped that there would be better attendance in future years. The program and speakers sounded inspiring to him.

Robert and Maud found a two-story brick house in New Wilmington; it was at 419 West Neshannock Avenue, with four bedrooms upstairs and a comfortable living room, dining room, and modern kitchen downstairs. The house had plenty of yard for a garden in the back and a porch and enough grass to toss a football in the front. It was only a quarter of a mile to the college and to New Wilmington Presbyterian Church and about the same distance to the stores and post office downtown on Neshannock and Market Streets.

The boys spent the summer working on the farm while their parents got things established in New Wilmington. They were immediately fascinated by the new place when they arrived. There were plenty of automobiles, and many places had electric lights. But there were also people who passed the house regularly in horse-drawn buggies and plain black or blue clothing. These were the Amish people who lived on farms all around the town and came in to sell their produce and baked goods and trade for the things they could not make themselves. They were Christian people whose interpretation of 2 Corinthians 6:14 taught them not to be "yoked together with unbelievers" and not to adorn their bodies unseemly. They did not have electricity on their property because the lines connected them to unbelievers. They used snaps and hooks and eyes instead of buttons on their clothing so as not to be showy in their manner of dress, and the women always covered their hair in modesty. The boys had seen many things and were familiar with many ways of worshipping God, but these plain Christian folks were new and interesting to them.

Once his family was well established and the boys all in school, the first two at Westminster and the others in public schools, Robert needed to get back to work. Maud's mother, Caroline, came up from Pittsburgh so that her daughter could travel to New York to see him off. Pictures at the ship show two tired-looking parents, standing side by side. It must have been a difficult goodbye after the too-short and hectic furlough. They were doing what they knew was best for their boys, but for themselves, it was impossible to know when and whether they'd be together again. Robert had his work in India, and Maud had the education of their four sons, which would not be finished before 1932. It might be a decade before they saw each other again, assuming both lived that long. On September 23, Robert wrote to Elizabeth from the SS *City of Lahore* to let her know he had gotten the communion set. He was sailing off the coast of Algeria at the time. He described the beauty of the moonlight on the water; the party gained a half-hour each day they sailed, and he looked forward to putting in at Port Sudan, where they would be joined by Dr. W. B. Anderson and Dr. C. S. Cleland, who would accompany Robert back to the field as they made a tour of the Punjabi mission and reviewed its work. Two Methodist women were on board from their Women's Board. They were very anxious about six of their missionaries from whom there had been no word before the ship sailed. They feared they may have died along with a hundred schoolgirls.

Most interesting by far to the boys left behind was the college, where George and Pollock began in September. There were fields on which Wallace and David could run and play after school and watch their big brothers at football practice. George and Pollok both tried out for the football team, along with about fifty other boys.

Football in those days was played with minimal pads and leather helmets. Both boys played on the team, and it was a rough sport. Years later, Pollock described a game in which so many of their team had been injured that they could only field ten in the last quarter. One reason for the injuries was that the linemen on the opposing team would drop down and roll into the Westminster boys. It was a very damaging tackle but apparently not illegal. Pollock, a lineman himself, began to drop on one knee as the tackle approached, timing it to catch the other player in the kidneys. After the game, one of the boys complain to him about his bruises. Pollock replied that he was just evening the odds and that he was sure the boy would live.

Football was a highlight of college for Pollock. During his senior year, the weekend they were to play their archrival, Geneva, he and several teammates decided to paint the opposing team's town blue. The freshman they sent to mix the paint used plaster of Paris, which had hardened by the time they were ready to paint. That plan nixed, they chose instead to roll the boulders that formed a G on the hillside overlooking the playing field into a W for Westminster. Dr. Wallace told him after the game that the president of Geneva had complimented him on the gentleman he was producing at Westminster, who showed such restraint in their antics the night before.

In 1924, the football program, and the athletic program in general, was greatly improved in Pollock's eyes when Jack Hulme joined the staff. Jack had been a boxer in his youth and went on to coach an

Olympic swim team shortly before he walked onto campus in the spring of 1924 for an interview with Dr. Wallace. Pollock had just had an argument with the president's secretary on a personal matter and was walking across campus, fuming, when Jack approached to ask the way to the Dr. Wallace's office. Pollock saw before him a man who looked like a bum. His nose slanted to one side, and he had a cauliflower ear, thanks to his boxing days. He looked like he had slept in his clothes, which he had; he was just walking up from the train.

Pollock delightedly took him to Dr. Wallace's secretary, just to see her reaction. His own reaction must have been fun to see when Jack produced a letter from Dr. Wallace, inviting him to campus regarding his application for a position with the athletics department. Jack became the trainer for the football team and the coach for swimming and gymnastics. Within eight years, he had 80 percent of the students engaged in some kind of athletic sport. But in the beginning, he was glad to make Pollock Maxwell his friend.

He was also glad to make the football team dig the swimming pool the college needed that summer. Digging out an Olympic-size pool became their primary conditioning exercise. When it was done, Jack told the well digger where he wanted the well for the pool, at the corner of the pool house. After arguing for a time that it was not a good location, the man drilled down two hundred feet and capped off what he was sure was a dry hole, just to show Jack. In the morning when Jack came to inspect, that cap was ten feet in the air. They had tapped into an artesian well. For years, the college sold water to the city of New Wilmington and offered free admission for city residents to the pool.

New Wilmington proved to be a happy place to live for the family. A college town, it offered good schools, a library, and interesting neighbors. There was always something to learn and something interesting to do. There were not the harsh winters of upstate New York, but there was plenty of snow in winter for sledding. The hill from the city hospital provided the best slope, and near the bottom, there was the exciting challenge of getting through the hospital gates at full speed without slamming into the brick wall surrounding the grounds. One day when the boys were sledding, David kept insisting that Pollock, who had him on his sled, let him take the hill by himself.

Finally worn down, against his better judgment. Pollock let him go. David sledded right down the hill and into the wall. His brother took him home for dead to their mother, but David was only unconscious and recovered from the concussion he suffered, with no lingering effects.

Pollock, who had always been accustomed to working and to making friends, continued to do both in New Wilmington. The whole family made friends with the Sharpe family, who operated a funeral home downstairs and lived upstairs with a big, boisterous crowd of children, some of whom were near the Maxwell boys in age. When the parents needed a babysitter, Pollock was glad to take on the job. The first time, he realized that even with three younger brothers, his skills were not as broad as he needed at the Sharpes, when the youngest needed changing. Keeping a level head in a crisis, he set up the ironing board near the wall phone, got a clean diaper and the baby, and called his mother. As she talked him through the job, he changed that boy on the ironing board; everyone had a good laugh about it for years afterward.

George took to Westminster eagerly. He knew he was headed for seminary after college and applied himself with that goal in mind. While in school, he met and fell in love with a classmate, beautiful, witty Katherine King, who would become his wife. Bright and hardworking, George finished at Westminster in three years and went on to seminary.

Pollock was less focused. He had no idea what he wanted to do with his life after college, but he knew that his family would be better off if he applied himself to earning as much money as he could while he was a student. One summer, and one summer only, he lived with his grandmother in Pittsburgh and worked in a steel mill. He later said it was the hardest work he ever did. That summer, he developed the ability to sweat profusely to survive the heat of the blast furnace. He called Caroline his little grandmother; at six feet one, when he held his arm out straight from his shoulder, she could walk under it without brushing the top of her head. His mother and the little boys came for a visit, and while they were there, Caroline collapsed, and Pollock carried her up to her bed. It was not a fatal illness, but it was a reminder to them all that Caroline was getting older. She lived to see Pollock graduate from college but died the following September of heart failure.

Pollock's more regular employment was manual labor in New Wilmington and on nearby farms. He helped Sharpe at the funeral home when an extra hand was needed, more for the meals upstairs

A Promised Life

than for monetary compensation. Mr. Sharpe was glad to have him, since not every strong boy is comfortable around a funeral home, and not every boy had Pollock's earlier work experience for the undertaker in New York. He did not mind the work. He also dug ditches as opportunity came up. One day, Dr. Wallace saw him digging a ditch and called him Tony (apparently, most ditch diggers he knew came from Italian families, and he liked to tease his cousin when he could). The name stuck. In the spring of 1927, Maud greeted Pollock when he walked into the house with the news that Dr. Wallace had just called and wanted to see him. Pollock went directly to the president's office, thinking it must be some last-minute instructions for the graduation ceremony where he was to act as junior marshal. Instead, what Dr. Wallace wanted was Pollock's word as a gentleman that he would make up the three hours he lacked that summer so he could graduate with his class. It was the college's seventy-fifth year, and they were graduating seventy-four.

After giving his word, Pollock went scrambling to find a mortar board and then flying home to get his mother to press his robe and her dress in time for his graduation.

His next job was one offered by Dr. Wallace. He was to be dean of freshmen and live in the freshmen dorm. Dr. Wallace explained that he was confident Tony would be the best man to know when the freshmen were up to something, since he had always been up to something himself. In this way, Pollock had the luxury of time to decide on his path while helping some younger men stay on theirs and be near enough to help his mother with young Wallace and David for a while longer.

***

On his return, Robert lived with the missionaries in the compound in Sialkot. When he got there, he was greeted by his sister Anna Belle's daughter, Margaret, who had been appointed to teach in the girls' school in Gujranwala; in time, she became the director, as her aunt, Maud, had been before her. Robert delighted in the chance to have family in India again and to get to know young Margaret as an adult. Her brother, George, and his wife, Cordelia, joined them in 1925 after George finished seminary. George's service was hampered by ill health, and he never returned from his first furlough, but the 1920s and early 1930s were a happier time for Robert because he had family nearby. He spent his first month back working on the deeds. It was work that had not been completed when he left for America for furlough. He was concerned about the situation of the missionaries, some of whom had not been paid the portion of their salaries owed by the presbytery for six months.

He was also concerned about Gordon College. Its senior faculty was mostly reassigned. With Dr. Mercer appointed the first general-secretary of the mission, Dr. Nesbitt reassigned to the seminary, and Dr. Mitchell on furlough, Robert was worried that the school was in the hands of younger, less experienced leadership and could suffer. He had great hopes for the new position of general-secretary. The responsibilities were beyond keeping minutes to being responsible for official communications with the foreign mission board on behalf of the Sialkot mission and for sharing reports with the wider church. Robert hoped that this change would mean better organization and communication than in the past.

Robert's own assignment was to Taxila Hospital. At Dr. Martin's request, he had been appointed as hospital superintendent. Hiring a nonmedical administrative superintendent would free the medical staff to practice medicine. Having the opportunity for evangelistic work with patients and staff as a part of the hospital team had real appeal for Robert. He was a natural choice, having been so intimately involved in the plans for building the hospital and having had much administrative experience with the boys' schools and the college. Dr. Martin asked that Robert be in place and well established before his own furlough the following year.

The letters from this period reflect a definite change in the attitude toward mission work in the American church. In one, Robert tells Dr. Anderson that he is relieved that the matter of Pentecostalism did not come up at a recent presbytery meeting. Apparently, Pentecostal zeal had inspired a few of the missionaries, but Robert was of the opinion and hope that it would soon die out, and the less said, the better. When they joined Robert on the SS *Lahore*, Dr. Anderson and Dr. Cleland were coming out to review the work in the field and report back. The late nineteenth-century zeal for missions, which had resulted in the great missionary movement, with its inspiring hymns like "We've a Story to Tell to the Nations," seemed to be flagging. Money was harder to raise. Demands for accountability for the work and justification for the expense in terms of concrete results were coming from many in the congregations and presbyteries in the States.

Dr. Anderson sent a copy of the initial draft of his report to Robert and other trusted missionary colleagues for their review and reflections. Robert responded in several pages of detail to the report. On church discipline, he said that it seemed wise to the missionaries not to be harsh in discipline, lest they drive people into the arms of the Roman Catholics. He reasoned that native pastors and elders in villages were better able to administer discipline than those in the cities like Sialkot, where word would spread and lead to general public shame. On salaries, he argued that unless a person, whether pastor or teacher, had a vocation such that they could do no other work than that to which they are called, the matter of a salary tempted those with no calling into the work for the money. With pastors, the hope was that as the mission kept salaries low, the congregations would supplement it, but he acknowledged that Anderson's caution that anyone should be paid such that they could live according to community standards was good counsel. On the matter of control of work by the Mission Executive Board, Robert felt that much more work was being delegated to committees and local boards. He was concerned, in fact, that the boards for women's schools and men's schools were functioning quite independently of the oversight of the executive board. The idea of having a general-secretary devoting all his time to the work seemed to be working out well.

The balance of mission and native Indian leaders in the decision-making process was difficult to achieve because busy native pastors and teachers did not want to take time away from their daily tasks for mission and presbytery committee work. He agreed that an independent audit of mission expenditures was due and noted that when all billing was dealt with by the general treasurer, audits of various stations would not be needed. The treasurer needed to be bonded, for his own protection and for the trust of the congregations and pastors.

Robert felt that mission schools needed to be evaluated in

comparison to government schools to see whether the dropout and failure rates were greater in one than the other. Farmer's son that he was, he remarked that like the odd jobs at harvest time wait for the wet day, this work was waiting for the opportune time, and he hoped the general-secretary would get someone on it quickly. He wrote of the failure of young men who completed a practical education course in going out to set up a business. He supported the suggestion of K. L. Kallia Ram that the missions combine to raise one hundred thousand rupees to allow farmers to buy land and repay the government in annual installments, as other farmers did. He felt that mission schools had lost their chance to be practical training schools in anything but Bible teaching. Regarding decision-making on matters in the mission, he felt that the best practice was for the responsible committee to present its recommendations to the full mission for action, so that all could be assured that they had ownership in decisions.

He responded to a comment about mission personnel, saying, "We need to have the Church at home hold us up in prayer continually. What a tragedy for men and women to leave their homes and come out here to become mere administrators trusting in anything but the direct intervention of the Creator."[30]

By February of 1925, as hospital administrator, Robert was gradually being handed the administrative work and deliberately took things slowly, as he was encouraged to do when the mission created the position. He helped to restore peace among conflicting parties at the hospital and instituted prayer meetings. Dr. Martin's wife graciously invited the senior staff to tea, and Robert and Dr. Martin consulted with the whole staff on how to improve things at the hospital. He was confident that enthusiasm for the work would soon replace the bitterness that had arisen. Robert requested Anderson to send a nurse as soon as possible for short-term work, preferably for five years. The hospital board had voted to employ two nurses as soon as a search could be completed for full mission terms. Miss Porter's contract for one nursing position was acceptable to the hospital board, which noted that she was paid a higher salary than most mission personnel because of her room and board provisions. Robert was confident that the mission would appoint her to a full term as director of nurses when she returned from furlough.

Dr. Martin wanted an assistant surgeon employed before he went on furlough. The Indian staff had had great turnover, and it was difficult to find replacement people who were single or able to accommodate themselves to available housing. The hospital was filled to capacity much of the time, and the housing for staff meant patients had to be turned away. With the warmer weather coming, they were concerned about the ability of one doctor to carry the load. Whether nurses should be regularly appointed long-term missionaries or contracted with the specific hospital continued to be a debate between the mission and the board. In celebration of the success of the hospital, the board released an additional fifteen thousand dollars for the third ward to be built that spring.

Dr. Anderson took ill in 1925, and Robert began a period of correspondence with H. C. Chambers, who filled in during his recovery. The two knew each other only by reputation, and their letters show that they worked very collegially together. Robert shared news of the hospital, and in each letter for several months, he urged Chambers to make finding a nurse for Taxila a top priority. In one, he described the position and the person wanted in detail: "We want a person who is able to get things done, able to get on with us who are older and more set in our ways, very keen about her profession, and one who has shown by her past life that she is a keen evangelist."[31] A matron to live in would make it possible to keep the women's department open, the women patients to feel that not only the doctors but also the nurses give them safe and quality care, and the two Indian nurses to feel safe living at the hospital. With Miss Porter away, the Indian nurses had to be given a month's vacation while the doctor was on summer leave and the women's department closed for the summer. He was constantly reassured that finding a nurse was a board priority and that there were several candidates to be interviewed. When the process was complete, a Miss Gailey was appointed for a five-year term to Taxila. She turned down an offer from a large American hospital to be director of nurses at a salary of twenty-eight hundred dollars in order to go to India. Chambers felt that the financial sacrifice was an indication of her missionary zeal.

In 1925, sadness struck the hospital community following a cholera epidemic. As many as thirty-five people a day died in Jhelum, and there were many deaths across the Punjab. One of those who died was Dr. J. W. Jongewaard, one of three members of a missionary family in service in the Punjab. She and her sister, a nurse, were on the staff of the hospital in Jhelum. Dr. Jongewaard reported that she felt ill at tea time one afternoon and believed she had contracted cholera. Her sister immediately sent for their brother. who was with Robert in Taxila, where he had been employed as assistant surgeon. By the time Dr. Jongewaard arrived from Taxila a little after midnight, his stricken sister did not recognize him, and she died the following morning. Cholera was a quick killer; there was little that could be done. The staff in Jhelum had not been inoculated in time against the disease, but the staff at Taxila had. They mourned with their friend who lost his sister and drove down to Jhelum for her funeral, but the Taxila Hospital was spared the worst of the epidemic that year.

In addition to his hospital work in these years, Robert was elected again as translating clerk of the Sialkot Synod and duly sent the minutes to the board. He was glad for reports that let him know that his worry about the seminary had been for nothing. The school was making good progress in training students and their wives for work in local village churches, both literate and nonliterate students, and was delighted with the emphasis placed on Bible memory work. He was perhaps even more glad that the synod was negotiating with the government for land for Christians to farm. He was sure their arguments to persuade the government to provide land below market value were sound and phrased to appeal to those granting land. They appealed on behalf of these lower caste persons noting that Christians had tilled the soil in the region for generations and would make the land produce.

He continued to be involved in trials of civil cases as well as church discipline in his work with the synod and reported news of trials to Chambers, with few details because the full matter would have been reported by the general-secretary of the mission. He was delighted to work with the synod leaders on a new printing of fifteen thousand copies of the Psalms to sell as part of the evangelistic work of congregations. The money from the sale would repay the loan from the synod. Translations of other texts for seminarians and pastors to help them think through how to approach their Hindu audience with the Gospel were being proposed, and Robert celebrated that effort.

A Promised Life

The Pentecostal spirit did not leave the mission easily. One of the women teachers especially had been granted the gift of the Spirit while home on furlough, and Robert was disappointed that she had been allowed to return to the field without a thorough investigation of what she intended. Apparently, she had intended to judge her colleagues who did not share her love for this relatively new phenomenon in American church culture and was causing distress and dissention in the field. Robert eagerly awaited the end of her term.

Even more vexing for mission personnel was the double taxation they paid each year, US income tax on money earned overseas and Indian tax on the same money. Robert and others appealed to the board, noting that the Methodists had found a way to offer some relief to their personnel. The Methodists paid husbands and wives separately and paid an educational stipends for children. The UPNA did not, and missionaries were taxed by the Indian government when they were on furlough in America as well as when they were in the field. The board acted to say that when wives are living in America, half of the salary would be declared for them and educational stipends for children would be nontaxable. Word of this action was conveyed to the mission treasurer, William Merriam, and to Rev. Mercer, the general-secretary. Robert was glad to get the news directly from Chambers, as well.

The years of work at the hospital were very satisfying for Robert and brought the facility a strong foundation of administrative support for its vital service to the frontier. Much remodeled and modernized, the hospital continues to serve into the twenty-first century at its original location between the road connecting Rawalpindi with Afghanistan and the railway station, still a grand location for a lifesaving service and Christian witness in that part of the world.

***

The late 1920s brought huge changes in the lives of all the Maxwells and of the larger world. In America, Wallace was finishing college and weighing whether law or ministry would be his calling. David was finishing high school and applying to Carnegie Tech for his engineering degree. Perhaps the biggest news belonged to Elizabeth;

after faithfully serving as her brother's partner in mission in America and her church and larger family as a single woman for years, in April 1928, at the age of sixty-two, she married her and Robert's first cousin, R. J. It was her only marriage and his third. They had been close friends since childhood, and their wedding picture shows a pair relaxed and comfortable, side by side. They would remain side by side in life until Elizabeth's death in 1942.

The next chapter for Robert would be a year of significant change, not only for his own work but for the American church and economy in general, as he moved from Taxila to Gujranwala in 1929, after his election as the second general-secretary of the mission.

CHAPTER

10

Making Do and Providing: 1929–1934

1929 brought a roller-coaster economy in the United States as a result of decreased postwar production and increased unemployment, which combined to produce overvalued stocks. The market hit a high in August that was unsustainable, and the instability led to a massive sell-off of stocks in late October, so that on October 29, the market crashed. US economic instability was part of a global economic decline. The Depression in America lasted from 1929 to 1939. By 1933, 30 percent of the workforce was unemployed, and half the banks had failed. Cities all over the country saw soup lines grow as many homeless folk, individuals and families, were unable to make enough to feed themselves. In 1934, America's heartland was devastated by drought. It became such a dust bowl that thousands left their farms and migrated west, looking for work. Roosevelt's administration put in place public works programs, particularly work on road infrastructure and buildings in cities and national parks, that helped mitigate the unemployment. It also put in place a reform in banking regulations to prevent another market crash.

In spite of all the government's efforts, the economy did not really begin to recover until the beginning of World War II, with its demand for goods. There were historic bright points in the midst of the gloom. In 1931, the Empire State Building, the tallest in the world at the time, was completed in New York. In aviation, Amelia Earhart became the first woman to complete a transatlantic flight in 1932, and the following year, Wiley Post flew around the world in eight and a half days. The same year, scientists first split the atom, and air conditioning was invented.

This same period saw rising political unrest in other nations and various measures to control sinking economies. In Europe, Austria, Poland, Czechoslovakia, Germany, France, Yugoslavia, and Bulgaria were the most severely hit by the Depression and were therefore not able to defend against Nazism when it came to them, first in Germany by election and in the other countries by invasion. In Soviet Russia under Stalin, collective farming replaced family farms and individual ownership of property. In 1933, Adolph Hitler was elected chancellor of Germany, and the first Nazi concentration camps were established.

***

India was a hotbed of political activity, as the people grew increasingly frustrated with British colonialism. In March 1930, Mohandas Gandhi led a two-hundred-forty-mile, twenty-four-day march to the Arabian Sea at Dandi, where his followers extracted their own salt from sea water. This began a nationwide boycott of the British salt tax. The march marked the beginning of the nonviolent, passive resistance protest that contributed a great deal to Indian independence seventeen years later. At that time, it was illegal to possess salt not purchased from the government. Salt was needed to flavor and preserve food. It was used for religious services, healing, disinfecting, and embalming. Since everyone needed salt, it was a cause that united Hindu, Muslim, Sikh, and Christian Indians, regardless of caste or class.

The economic decline and the political unrest both influenced mission work in India greatly in this period, and Robert, as the new general-secretary of the Sialkot mission, had his work cut out for him. He was forever negotiating funds to cover mission expenses with an American church that had less and less money to spend. He was working with an Indian church eager for increasing control of its own life and missionaries anxious about letting go of control of the evangelistic work and of the limited funds to support it. He was

A Promised Life

working with others to draft policies to be sure that mission schools were in compliance with more and more stringent government standards. These same mission leaders were negotiating with the government to continue schools so that boys and girls could get the education they needed to be able to contribute to society and provide for their families, regardless of their background.

He was especially grateful for his friend, William H. Merriam, general treasurer of the mission, with whom he could regularly confer on the challenges before them. For part of the time while Robert was general-secretary, the Merriam family welcomed him as a member of their household, and those conferences were an every-evening event. He was also grateful for his even older friend, Dr. Anderson, at the foreign mission board, who always understood the reason for requests, even if they couldn't always be granted. A deep joy of this season was the fact that he had family in the field. Margaret's brother, George Murdoch, and his wife, Cordelia, had a little son. Christmas was a special time for Robert and the Murdochs to celebrate together. George Murdoch's work in ministry gave Robert a window into what life must be like for George and Katherine Maxwell, as they began life in marriage and ministry together back in the States.

Robert quickly learned that having communication go through the general-secretary had its limitations. He was criticized by some at the board for writing to Dr. Anderson about matters that were the business of the treasurer, not the secretary. He apologized and asked Dr. Anderson in future to help him remember to refer all such matters to Merriam.

When there was need for additional teachers at Woodstock School and at Kinard College, he sent what he thought were explicit instructions to Miss Milligan, the staff member at the board in charge of recruiting teachers. With mail taking three to four weeks to go one way, he soon found that although he thought he had been clear and complete, he was mistaken. Months of correspondence later, teachers were selected who were not prepared to teach the subjects needed, and in one case especially, Miss Milligan was furious and embarrassed when it fell to her to break a contract. It took careful diplomacy on Robert's part, both with her and with the heads of the schools, to find

115

a way through to discover qualified candidates acceptable both to the boards of the schools and to the foreign mission board.

Communication was made more challenging when Dr. Anderson was released to go into the church to raise money for the mission, which was only natural, since he was a much-beloved figure throughout the church. His work correspondence was taken up by Dr. Mills Taylor, who had previously been in charge of the development work Dr. Anderson would now be doing. Dr. Taylor was not especially familiar with the mission in India. Robert found himself explaining how and why the work was done as it was. He found it was a mistake every time he reverted to the shorthand correspondence that Dr. Anderson knew so well, but Dr. Taylor had no way to understand. The arrangement did not last for many months. Dr. Anderson was diagnosed with a serious throat condition that made travel impossible. He was able to do office work and so returned to his desk.

Regarding Dr. Anderson's diagnosis, Robert wrote to him, "We cannot understand but we can trust Him implicitly and delight in the loving kindnesses which He showers upon us all our days."[32]

The missionaries and the Indian church leaders saw the impact of economic decline directly. Schools had to be closed for lack of funds to pay teachers. Evangelistic work was curtailed because there were fewer missionaries in the field to train native workers. Every year, the missionaries held their collective breath until news came of the board's decisions about who would be sent out and who would be retained in America following furlough. In 1930, there was no language school at Landour because no new missionaries were sent out. Pay for Indian teachers and evangelistic workers was a hotly debated topic. The women teachers had had a regular pay scale in place for years, but not the men, and it was recommended that a scale with regular review be put in place and used before salaries were increased. Evangelistic workers went to seminary in some cases because grants were more than they could make working; they stayed in the field for years without establishing a self-supporting congregation. The mission felt this practice needed to be better controlled, especially since there was no way to know what these workers were paid by congregation members in addition to their mission salaries.

The Sialkot Synod established a standard that all village

evangelistic workers needed to be able to teach Bible. The residence at Boys' Industrial School in Gujranwala became available for the general-secretary. Two rooms were wired for electricity, a treat for the secretary, who had not had electric lighting in his home in India before 1929, but the building itself was in bad repair. Many other buildings (some of them built in the mid-1850s) were in desperate need of repair. The parsonage at Jhelum was so damaged in the flood of 1928 that the family was living in a tent a year later. The tent replaced by the Sialkot mission for its convocation was purchased for the boys' school, as the boys need some place to sleep when the missionaries took over their dormitory for synod meetings. Funds for repairs came from the sale of closed schools; there was no alternate source of funding.

The medical mission established its own careful policies to keep costs to a minimum. These policies included that a hospital should have two physicians, one to serve as superintendent if a nonmedical superintendent is not employed, and a director of nurses, as the total non-Indian professional staff, with additional staff paid by the income from the hospital. In no case was there to be a hospital established in a community that already had a hospital. Mission-sponsored hospitals were for the purpose of providing medical care to people who otherwise would not have it.

As ever, Robert saw in the natural world signs of God's faithfulness and reasons for trust and hope. On February 6, 1930, he wrote to Anderson, "Monday summer got the better of winter and spring began."

For their part, Dr. Anderson and the foreign mission board were working hard to find new and creative ways to renew the church's interest in funding the missions. The board contracted with Mr. Willard Price to promote mission work in India and the Sudan. Price was a well-respected photographer and journalist who for six years edited *World Outlook*, the magazine of the New World Mission Movement, until that interdenominational movement ended.

He arrived on February 25, 1930, to take pictures and gather interviews for articles in the United Presbyterian denominational magazine and *Missionary Review of the World*, another Christian magazine with wider circulation. He visited the Boys' Industrial

Home in Gujranwala, Gordon College in Rawalpindi, the Christian Training School in Sialkot, and the hospital in Taxila. He was part of the eightieth birthday celebration of Miss R. A. McCullough, a missionary teacher still active in the field. His trip also included visits to village churches and schools and pictures of Hindu shrines. He must have been impressed with what he saw of the field. He took more than two hundred photos instead of the forty he had planned to take, and his articles with their accompanying pictures told the story of what was going on in the field far more convincingly than missionary statistical reports ever could.

The board was also doing everything it could to provide for missionaries in difficult times. In 1930, a pension plan for missionaries was established; missionaries could voluntarily enroll in the plan, contributing a portion of their salaries to be invested to provide for their retirement years. Robert enrolled as early as was possible and faithfully reported each missionary who wished to be added to the plan. Provision for retirement was timely. As the Depression continued, missionary salaries were reduced from $1,750 per year to $1,050. For all missionaries, this reduction was a real hardship. For missionaries like Robert, maintaining two homes on his salary, it was close to impossible.

In 1929, the mission and the Sialkot Synod adopted a set of policies written by their joint committee on closer mission/church relations. The policies included the following:

> The church is an autonomous and fully independent body. As missionaries, we recognize that our allegiance and service are due primarily to the church. The mission organization is secondary and temporary. The church is primary and permanent.
>
> Our purpose is to establish a church that shall not only be entirely independent and autonomous, but fully self-supporting and self-propagating.
>
> It is the work of Presbytery to exercise ecclesiastical jurisdiction and control over all congregations and unorganized groups of Christians

within its bounds, and over pastors and evangelists serving them.

The missionaries should function as members of congregations or of Presbyteries in all their relations to the work of congregations and Presbyteries.[33]

The policies were adopted to further strengthen the independence of the Indian church, which was seventy-five years old that year. Putting these policies in practice, however, was not always easy. Sometimes, the Indian leaders let it be known that they really did not want the responsibility of detailed accounting and decisions about financing work. They wanted to be free to lead worship and teach the Bible. Sometimes, the missionaries worried that things would fall apart if they did not maintain control of administration of ministry and funding. The general-secretary and treasurer and older, wiser heads invariably raised the question of how a church could be truly independent unless its Indian leaders took responsibility for administrative leadership. With the missionaries, they asked whether they would not be glad for the freedom from administrative responsibility, which would grant them time for the evangelistic work they came to India to do, work that had gotten swallowed up in the daily tasks of administration.

Merriam patiently reminded people that he needed receipts (or at least proof of approval) for expenses before he could release funds. Robert prayed for patience and good humor for them both as they dealt with anxious people all around. The people had good reason to be anxious. The changes they were undertaking were huge and risky. They had no way to know what funds would be available for work in the year ahead, and several times in the 1930s, there were budget cuts of 15 and 20 percent. They had no way of knowing how the political situation would work itself out or how long they would be working together in the years ahead.

The political situation in India worried the people supporting mission work back home in America. The missionaries on furlough wondered whether their wives and children should return with them. In May of 1930, Anderson wrote to say that the board was watching the papers closely for news from India and praying for the safety of missionaries. The morning paper on May 2 had reported that European women and children in the Punjab had been instructed to begin moving into the British forts. The conflict had risen to the point that Anderson referred to it as revolution in his letter. Robert's letter in reply assured Anderson that the conference held at Satyagraha, which included the president of the National Indian Congress and other leaders, passed off peacefully, as far as he knew.

On May 5, the American papers reported Gandhi's arrest. Gandhi is credited as the father of the Indian independence movement, which involved nonviolent protests leading toward an independent India with religious pluralism. Robert felt Gandhi was right in blaming the police for provoking a lot of the violence at demonstrations in the cities in protest of the salt tax, but there were inflamed passions and provocations on both sides, including people boarding trains en masse without paying and rioting in the cities. In 1942, Gandhi's vision of a peaceful, pluralistic India was challenged by the demand for a separate Muslim state in the Punjab. Ultimately, Indian independence in 1947 resulted in the partition into Pakistan, India, and what is now Bangladesh. Gandhi was arrested many times by the British for his leadership in the independence movement and the social disturbance that resulted.

In a letter May 19, Robert wrote to Anderson, "Many thanks for the sheets of the Civil and Military Gazette. It is good to get such a look at ourselves through the eyes of others sometimes. The writer might have said some things that would have reflected very much more seriously on America and her attitude toward the race problem. That would not have done his cause any good, however, for Indians would simply have charged the whole business up against the white race. We have something coming to us on that score."[34]

In June, Robert and Merriam were called into the city police station to give information about Indian Christians, who were among the most vocal advocates of independence. The two mission leaders were asked to keep the authorities apprised of any information they had about troublemakers, and the authorities assured them that information would flow from them, as well. The missionaries were assigned places of rendezvous in the event of uprisings.

The missionaries were more plagued by fact-finding visits and surveys from the American churches than they were troubled by danger to their physical health from Indian uprisings. During Robert's two-year term as general-secretary, the American Christian churches wanted to know that the money they were spending on mission was actually making a difference. Two different groups sent surveys and visitors to the Sialkot mission to study the situation in the field. The missionaries resented the time away from their work the visits demanded and were not as detailed and diligent as might have been helpful in the taking of surveys. It must have been difficult for them to know that the economic situation at home, half a world away, was making people there very anxious about contributing their money for missions, since there was so much need at home.

Detailed statistical studies became increasingly popular in the 1920s and 1930s as a way of measuring the effectiveness of a wide range of activities. The application of statistical studies to compare the effectiveness of various mission fields and develop standards did not sit well with missionaries who recognized, as they thought those studying them did not, that different regions and different cultures responded differently to the Gospel. They knew that the church in India was growing as rapidly as it could, while over the Khyber Pass in Afghanistan, Christian mission was forbidden, so the spread of the Gospel there was in secret if at all and could not be measured. When the results of the surveys were announced, the Sialkot mission was seen in a very positive light, but the process of getting there was stressful.

The general-secretary's own statistical report for 1930 paints a picture of an active church supported by an active mission. There were 111 organized congregations and 317 other places of regular worship, with eighty-three unorganized circles of evangelistic work. Seventy-six congregations had pastors, and thirty-five were served by supplies or licensed candidates for ordination in the Sialkot Synod. In the high schools, there were 1,949 non-Christian students and a total enrollment of 2,352. The total number of students in all schools, primary through higher education, was 12,066.

Following his term as general-secretary, Robert returned to educational work. He was assigned to manage the high school in Abbottabad, where he wished for Dr. Anderson's facility with Arabic and his ability to charm Muslims. He often thought of Dr. Anderson's work in the founding of Gordon College. In the year that Robert spent in Abbottabad, Dr. Anderson was elected moderator of the General Assembly back home in America. Robert knew it was a fitting honor for a man who had devoted his adult life to the church and the Gospel. When he wrote to congratulate him, he said he was confident that the church was in good hands and was grateful that Dr. Anderson was healthy enough to serve in this way.

It was a difficult year away from his friends in the field. Abbottabad was 190 miles from Gujranwala, so regular quick visits were out of the question. Shortly after he arrived there, two mission friends, Dr. W. T. Anderson and his son, Maurice, died the same week (Maurice from accidental gunshot). Robert wondered what the widows would do. He wrote to Dr. W. B. Anderson (no relation) that he wondered whether the difficulties faced by the church were due to the forgetfulness of God. He hoped that what people forgot in prosperity, they would remember in adversity.

The lack of interest in world evangelism by the Home Missions people in India seemed to have left them in dire straits. He worried that neither the American church nor the Indian church was as supportive of the missions as they needed in order to continue. In addition to his work at the school, Robert had been assigned to continue working on deeds and property records for the mission and to deal with cases of discipline before the presbytery and synod. After being part of the judicial commission dealing with an appeal of the defrocking of two ministers by Sialkot presbytery for adultery, he was annoyed with those leaders who failed to follow the rules and allowed the defendants to file an appeal.

After a year, Robert was reassigned to the high school in Rawalpindi, the school he served when he first came out to India. He shared a house there with Jim and Dorothy Cummings, both children of missionaries. Jim Cummings was appointed in 1924 and served at Gordon College. No missionary was appointed to take Robert's place at Abbottabad. There were a thousand boys at the high school in Abbottabad, and after Robert left, it was managed totally by Indian staff.

Toward the end of the year, Robert was very concerned about

A PROMISED LIFE

the future of the Rawalpindi school. It continued to be strong and to attract students, but he feared it would be closed at the end of the academic year in March. The question before the mission was whether itinerant evangelism or maintaining the school was of more benefit for Christian witness.

***

Meanwhile, back in the United States, life moved on in spite of the economic trials. Elizabeth settled into the life she shared with R. J. She found less time to write and no need to save letters any longer. The boys were becoming men. George spent a year at Allegheny Seminary before transferring to Princeton. In 1929, George was ordained, and he and Katherine were married. He served as assistant pastor at Vance Church in Wheeling, West Virginia, from 1929 to 1931 and then was called as pastor at the Waynesburg, Pennsylvania, church. Their daughter Nancy was born there in 1932, the first of Maud and Robert's ten grandchildren.

Pollock remained at Westminster, keeping an eye on the newest students. He considered teaching and worked toward a master's in history at Ohio State before leaving the college in 1932 to enter Princeton Seminary. In the summer of 1930, Maud began correspondence with Dr. Anderson in which she asked for Wallace to be allowed to go to India for a year with his father to help him decide between law and ministry. When the request was denied, she sounded angry and confused in her response, saying that "some families" had adult children go out to India "but not others." Dr. Anderson patiently explained that the board sent an adult daughter when the mother was absent or dead to be housekeeper for her father, but in no other circumstances.

In a July letter in 1930, Robert reported on the births of three children to missionaries, including a daughter to George and Cordelia Murdoch. He sent a cablegram for news of his family that summer, and Maud replied to Dr. Anderson's letter, which told her of the cablegram. She was very embarrassed and annoyed. They had been ill, she with pneumonia, for a time Pollock was sent home from school with what was feared to be scarlet fever but turned out to be sunburn.

123

They had all been busy with celebrating Wallace's college graduation. Maud was annoyed with Robert, and she told Dr. Anderson he could tell him that her sister, Nell, was still alive so Robert could rest assured that if someone died, he would be informed. She said that when a man puts half a world between himself and his family, he should not get panicky when he does not hear.

At this point, Robert and Maud had been half a world apart for twelve years, and the stress of raising four sons alone on very little money was showing. It would have been impossible except that both the college and the seminary provided very generous scholarship assistance to the children of ministers and missionaries. She managed to raise them and educate them, but it was a constant worry for her.

As the Depression deepened and salaries were cut while her sons completed graduate education, Maud pinched every penny she could to have something to send to them. For a long time after David went to Carnegie Technical Institute, with Wallace in law school at Duke and Pollock at Princeton in seminary, Maud survived on a diet consisting mainly of tea and toast. By January of 1934, her health had deteriorated to the point that her children were very concerned about her. She was both physically weak and mentally confused that winter. She spent time in Waynesburg with George and Katherine, and the doctor there thought the best thing for her was to return to India.

When Robert learned of her condition, he asked Dr. Anderson to arrange treatment for her at Columbia Hospital in New York, and Maud made the same request. She spent several weeks at Columbia, where doctors evaluated her psychological condition as well as her physical health. With a nourishing diet and rest, she was restored to her usual good health and left the hospital with a diagnosis of anemia of the brain due to lack of nutrients. When she left, Pollock took the train from Princeton up to New York to get her to spend a little time with him before she went home.

She was to meet his fiancée in Princeton. Pollock and Leaschen Wells were to be married on Robert's birthday, August 14, that summer. He was nervous about the meeting and nervous about his mother's condition. After her discharge, as they walked down the street chatting, Maud asked him to cross the street. Puzzled, he asked why. She replied that she did not want to encounter the man who was approaching them, and Pollock told her he was sure she did not know him. To show her son she was right, she continued down the sidewalk until the man stopped them to speak. She introduced Pollock, and they continued on their way. When they were well out of his hearing, Maud firmly explained to Pollock that she had not wanted to speak to the man because she had known him and his reputation on the mission field, and his loose morals made him someone she would rather avoid. Pollock decided that his mother's mind was fine and stopped worrying about the impression she would make on Leaschen.

That spring, Maud saw Wallace graduate from Duke and David from Carnegie Tech. With her children grown and self-supporting, Maud was more than ready to return to Robert in India. First, the board had to hear from her doctor in New York that she was really fit to return. Initially, the board recommended that Robert come home for a year to be reacquainted with his wife before they returned to India. That recommendation did not suit either Maud or Robert. Robert offered instead to forego any further furlough and not return to America until he reached mandatory retirement age in 1941.

The board finally agreed. The delay meant that Maud was in the States for Pollock's wedding at the Wells' home in Cairo, West Virginia. Finally, since no other missionaries were scheduled to travel so late in the year, on November 27, she sailed alone from New York for Marseilles on the *Excalibur* and transferred to the *Rawalpindi*, arriving in Bombay on December 27.

CHAPTER
11

A Promise Kept: 1935–1946

In 1934, Christmas was an extended holiday for Robert. Maud arrived on December 27, and once more they took the trip north to the Sialkot mission compound together, filled with joy at finally being reunited and with memories of that first trip north from the ship when they were just starting out. The house in Sialkot brought many memories. Dr. Anderson had written in his bon voyage letter to Maud that when Dr. Barr lived there, he had threatened to tie a bell on his wife so he would be able to find her, the place was so big. They remembered when they raced ahead of the welcoming party for Dr. Anderson to be at the house to welcome him back. Robert smiled at the memory of soiling his sleeve with chocolate pudding that Christmas, such a laughably embarrassing impression. He reminded Maud of the time when he acted as vice president for Dr. Anderson when that good man lay in bed in that house, too ill with fever to go about his work. It was in that house that Dr. Stewart, a few hours before his death, commissioned Robert to secure the title to the site for the seminary. It was there that Dr. Crowe lay ill with fever while Robert and Dr. Caldwell tried to care for him, and Dr. Caldwell burned incense to clear the mosquitoes out of the house's magnificent rooms during Robert's first summer on the plains. The house was full of memories, and Maud was back with him to make more. They were having the time of their lives being together again.

Robert was back to devoting himself to education and evangelism for the most part, after his time as general-secretary of the mission. He served as treasurer at the Christian Training Institute in Sialkot, with Hakim Din as principal of the school. Dr. Anderson, Dr. Campbell, and Dr. Barr had all served at the institute in earlier years and occupied the house where Maud and Robert now lived. Maud took on running the school dispensary and was very popular with the boys, who seemed to Robert to prefer going to be treated at the dispensary to attending classes. The other missionary staff at the school were Robert Foster and his wife. Mrs. Foster was the daughter of W. T. Anderson and grew up in the mission. The Fosters were devoted to the development and training of the boys, who would spread the gospel in due time as evangelists, teachers, and pastors when their education was complete. Bob Foster was the scout leader at the school. He entered into the boys' games and knew them well. He took twenty-five scouts from the district to meet Lord Robert Baden-Powell, the founder of Boy Scouting, at the scout jamboree in New Delhi, when Baden-Powell visited India. In the winter of 1935, the water tank was rebuilt, and the boys, one class a day, were able to enjoy themselves in the bathing tank that Dr. Campbell built.

Robert felt that Hakim Din did well as principal of the school. He had a love for the boys and the work, and when necessary, he had great tact in selecting the ablest students for advanced work instead of selecting boys from wealthy families with fathers who insisted on the promotion, even if their boys were less equipped for the work. Robert wondered what the effect would be on his work if Din was elected to the Legislative Council of the Punjab, which he very much hoped to be. Din hired two cars to bring people to the polls to vote for him during the three-week election season. With 190 boarders splashing in the tank in the winter of 1935, Robert knew Din would have his work cut out for him winnowing the number down to a manageable 150 for the next year.

Robert's correspondence during this period was more relaxed, filled with school news and humorous stories he knew Dr. Anderson would enjoy. One story that made them both chuckle was the gift of twenty-five dollars sent from a church in Ohio for the education that year of Hakim Din. Din, the school's principal, had already received a fine education in mission schools and was now glad to see that other boys had a chance to experience the education that served him so well. It only took Merriam a month to straighten out with the donors the true purpose of the gift so that it could be applied to educate a current student.

Robert clearly was happy to let Merriam, Dr. Chambers, and others have the bulk of the administrative tasks. There were still areas that demanded his attention beyond the Christian Training Institute. The board wanted a valuation of all the mission's property, and Robert's 1929 list of properties was not complete. His help was needed to establish the current value of those properties he listed, a task he observed to Dr. Anderson would be much easier in the States than in India, where it was difficult to get anyone to give an estimate of a property not for sale and where valuations fluctuated widely, depending on who one asked.

He was elected statistician by the mission and had the job of collecting reports from each of the congregations, schools, and hospitals in the mission for the General Assembly report each year. The Sialkot mission stretched from the Afghan border in the north south to Lyallpur (350 miles), and from the Sargodha area in the west to Pathankot in the current-day Punjab area of India in the east (217 miles) in a strange L-shaped area of around thirty thousand square miles. Robert was statistician from 1935 until 1940, when the mission wisely gave the job to someone else while Robert was still in the field, to offer advice and counsel before leaving to retire in America.

The statistical report for 1935 shows that in the eighty years since the work began, the mission and its converts had not been idle:

Category	Total Number
Evangelistic workers	256
Ordained men	128
Nonordained men	84
Women	44
Presbyteries in synod	7
Congregations	124
Self-supporting	112

Worshipping groups	53
Church members	43,482
Current year professions	2,725
Sunday schools	108
Students	4,637
Youth societies	25
Members	893
Educational institutions	118
Students	10,063
Christian students	3,797
Medical work	
Hospitals	5
Medical dispensaries	8
Hospital beds	222
Patients current year	3,136
Surgeries current year	497
Doctors	11
Missionary doctors	3
Native doctors	8
Annual income from Indian sources	113,664
Educational	75,542
Indian church	14,586
Medical	13,615
Industrial work	981
Sale of Bible tracts	236

35

By 1937, in addition to being the statistician for the Sialkot mission and being promoted to vice-principal of the Christian

Training Institute, Robert was secretary of the Sialkot Convention, which held a meeting each year at the Sialkot mission for prayer and lectures by invited speakers. He was the only male missionary for Lyallpur (today's Faisalabad) and Sangla Hill, due west of Lahore and about twenty miles apart, and a hundred sixty miles from Sialkot. He rode the train a lot. He was delighted when the minister of education visited CTI and made complimentary remarks about the school. The minister said he had received all of his education in mission institutions and that the government was not ungrateful for what the missions had done in education and medical work.

It was gratifying to hear a positive word from a government officer. It was difficult to know how the government transition would go and what it would mean for the mission and its work. It seemed increasingly unlikely that a one-India solution was possible with Hindus, Muslims, and Sikhs together. The mission schools had had success with educating boys and girls from all those backgrounds in the same school, but they were a small percentage of a vast subcontinent, and the reports in the papers did not give a lot of hope. Even if a transfer of power to one Indian government were possible, it remained to be seen whether the schools and hospitals would stay in the hands of the Indian church or whether they would become the property of the new government.

Robert and Maud never heard enough from their boys to suit them, but they did hear when Pollock's son, Robert Nelson, was born in July 1935 and when David married Kathryn Seaman in Philadelphia in October of that year. Pollock had enjoyed his years in seminary and, determined that he was called to ministry, did not return to Westminster College. He knew that his father would find it ironic that the son of a man who chose not to attend seminary at Princeton because of its eating clubs was earning his meals working as steward for one of those clubs, Benham. In addition to food, that job had other perks. Pollock got to know Albert Einstein, who lived between the seminary and Benham and who was glad for Pollock's invitations to join the club for dinner whenever pistachio ice cream was on the menu for dessert. After graduation, Pollock wrote to his parents that he was working in Pikeville, Kentucky, doing educational work for the Board of Christian Education of the Presbyterian Church USA. David and

Kay both worked for the Philadelphia Relief Board. Wallace was in the Alcohol Control Bureau in Washington DC, and George was at the Presbyterian Church in Waynesburg. A year later, David was working in Washington, while Kay remained in Philadelphia until she, too, could find work in Washington. George performed the wedding of Wallace and his bride, Margaret Goldberg, who joined him in Washington. George and Katherine in Waynesburg welcomed a second daughter, also Margaret. With a growing family back in the States, Robert wondered from time to time whether he had been selfish in asking to be retained in India, especially when so many of his missionary friends were not able to return following furloughs. He and Maud did not know what work they would be fit for in the States, however, and so they carried on, confident that there would be time to get to know these new daughters and grandchildren in their retirement years.

In 1938, Dr. Anderson retired from the board. He had served faithfully and well in sickness and in health for many years. Robert and Maud knew that his retirement was well earned, but Robert would sorely miss their regular correspondence, with the chance it brought to reflect with one who knew well just what was behind what Robert was saying. Dr. Anderson had been there himself and knew what life in India was like. Robert wrote to say that he and Maud would forever be grateful to Dr. Anderson and his wife, Blanche, for the care with which they introduced them to mission life and for their friendship across the years. The same year, Dr. and Mrs. Chambers retired from the field. Merriam became both general-secretary and treasurer for the mission in addition to his heavy responsibilities at Gordon College. Bob Foster was ill on furlough, and they did not yet know whether he would return. Robert observed that they were rather few in the field.

***

While life continued in relative peace and joy for Robert and Maud in Sialkot, the larger world marched toward global war. In 1937, Japan invaded China, and armed conflict between the two went on in mainland China and in Burma until the conclusion of World War II. Germany continued its push into neighboring states weakened by the Depression. It sent increasing numbers of people to the concentration camps: Jews from all those countries as well as others judged defective, German Christian leaders, and others who opposed the Nazi Reich. In 1938, President Franklin Roosevelt called a summit of leaders from thirty-two nations, who met in France to discuss increasing immigration of German Jews. In the end, only the Dominican Republic increased their quota of Jewish immigrants. This contributed to the Nazi belief that no one wanted the Jews. The alternative solution of extermination followed.

On September 1, 1939, Germany invaded Poland. Two days later, Great Britain and France, which had treaties with Poland, declared war on Germany. Germany continued its invasion, moving on Luxemburg, Belgium, and the Netherlands and ultimately conquering France. In three months, Germany completed its conquest of Western Europe and set its sights on the British Isles. Britain held out. Churchill asked for and received support from the United States in terms of arms, food, and supplies. Germany invaded the Soviet Union, disregarding their no-aggression pact, and now Germany fought a war on two fronts. In the vast Soviet territory, under Stalin's orders, farmers burned crops and killed livestock as they fled, forcing the Germans to rely on their own supplies. Albert Einstein wrote to President Roosevelt that year from Princeton to inform him of the possibility of building an atomic bomb to use against the Germans.

On December 7, 1941, the Japanese bombed Pearl Harbor in Hawaii, sinking and damaging much of the US Pacific fleet; the United States declared war on Japan and, three days later, on Germany. In May 1945, Germany surrendered after the Allied push from North Africa through France, Austria, and Italy and from Russia into Germany. In April, the Russian forces had Berlin, the German capital, completely surrounded. Germany surrendered on May 7. Roosevelt had died on April 12, and Harry Truman was president. The atomic bomb was developed and used against Japan after the European war ended. Japan surrendered on September 2, ending the war in the Pacific. Hoping to prevent total war from ever happening again, on October 24, 1945, representatives from fifty nations met in San Francisco and formed the United Nations.

***

A Promised Life

Once again, just as in 1918, when the Maxwells contemplated going home to America, the world beyond them was facing the chaos of war. The mission approved Robert's request to be retired on his seventieth birthday, August 14, 1941. He and Maud would stay on in retirement until the spring of 1942, when they would return to America.

Dr. Taylor, Dr. Anderson's successor, had visited the field with his wife in earlier years, when he was working at the board. He wrote a personal word when he wrote in response to Robert's letter to request the board to concur with the mission's action on his retirement. Dr. Taylor said, "Knowing how useful a man you have been in the field and what a hole it will make in things when you leave, I trust that both you and Mrs. Maxwell will have the health and strength you need to the end of your period of service. Mrs. Taylor and I will never forget your many kindnesses to us. Those hours live in our memories as among the most delightful in our life."[36]

Dr. Reed, with whom Robert corresponded regularly about statistics and property values, also recognized Robert's value to the work. He wrote to let Robert know that the board had voted to confirm his retirement as he requested.

Dr. Reed said, "I know that I speak for the Board when I express deep appreciation of your contribution to the life of the Mission and the Church in India. Many of the tasks that you have carried out have been of the type which are arduous without giving much evidence of reward. Nevertheless, you have performed them willing and well. It is our prayer that God may continue to bless you, enriching your last months of service in India and giving you more years of usefulness to the Church both in India and in America subsequent to your retirement."[37]

Robert and Maud began to celebrate annual events for the last time in India. In March of 1941, they attended the commencement at Gujranwala Theological Seminary. The Rev. Andrew Thakur Das of the United Church of Northern India, whose father was earlier a professor at the seminary, gave a commencement address that the Maxwells enjoyed very much. As a part of the exercises, all twenty-two graduates preached. Most of them preached to small groups, but two were chosen to preach to the graduation audience. No one had told them how long to preach. One preached for forty-five minutes and the other for fifty. Several members of the board were asleep by the time they finished. Robert managed to stay awake but thought to himself that the preachers, though they gave valuable instruction, overestimated the congregation's ability to absorb it.

He was glad that Bob Foster was well enough to return to India for the final years of Robert's time at the Christian Training Institute. Mrs. Foster's mother, Mrs. W. T. Anderson, stayed in India following her husband's death. When she visited the Fosters for the last time before the Maxwells left, all enjoyed a station dinner at the Fosters that was rather hilarious. Mrs. Anderson had always been vivacious at parties, and the young missionary women in Sialkot studying the language seemed to enjoy the evening as much as the aged ones did.

***

As the United States entered the war, the next generation of Maxwells made plans for their own participation in the war effort. Three of Robert and Maud's four sons enlisted in the military as the United States entered the war. Wallace joined the Navy and was posted to the North Atlantic on supply ships. Later, he was posted to Washington, where his legal training and earlier experience in DC made him invaluable in the judge adjutant general's office.

George accepted a call to Mt. Lebanon Presbyterian Church in Pittsburgh in 1941 and determined that his best service was to continue serving there.

Pollock and Leaschen's marriage did not survive a move to north Alabama to serve a church in Sheffield; they divorced in January 1940. He sent his parents the news and her address so that they could continue to stay in touch with four-year-old Bobby. In April, he married Muriel Owen, a nurse who helped treat the bleeding ulcers that resulted from the stress of his failed marriage. She was an Alabama native and easily fit into the role of pastor's wife. In December 1941, Pollock told her that he could not send men off to war and stay home. He enlisted in the Army as a chaplain. David followed his eldest brother into the Army, enlisting in May 1942.

Robert's health was not good in his last months in the field. By the time he and Maud left early in 1942, his doctor was very concerned about him and did not think he was strong enough for winter weather in New Wilmington. Fortunately, by then, Pollock and Muriel were in Pensacola, Florida, where Pollock was preparing for service with the 82nd Division in the European theater of war under the command of General Omar Bradley. He would report directly to General Geoffrey Keyes, and as General Keyes rose in rank and responsibility, he wanted his chaplain with him near the front. In the winter and spring of 1942, Pollock and Muriel were delighted to welcome Robert and Maud to Pensacola. Muriel nursed both of them, insisting on good nutrition, which she provided, and rest as well as walks on the beach to enjoy the ocean air. Muriel's parents had both died when she was still a girl, so she felt as though Pollock's parents were in part hers now, as well. Robert and Maud found that they loved this new daughter-in-law, with her thoughtful ways and soft Southern voice. Her care proved to be just what they needed. By the time Pollock was off with his troops to south Louisiana for training in preparation for leaving, they were ready to head for New Wilmington, with a stop to see George and Katherine and meet those granddaughters in Pittsburgh first.

***

The years in New Wilmington were filled with happy reunions, even in the midst of war. Friends from the mission field had retired there, and those who had not always came for Mission Conference in the summer. George and Katherine and the girls visited. Bobby's picture was prominent on the mantle, along with theirs. Wallace and Margaret gave them another grandson, another Robert, and a granddaughter, Anne. David and Katherine gave them Gayle and Jed. There was not work for them to do, but they did not want work to do. They lived simply on the retirement funds the board provided, with some help from their sons from time to time. There was not much money for anybody, and everyone lived with ration books for goods and self-sacrifice for the war effort. Robert had the college library available whenever he wanted to walk over. Maud thrived on the life of the congregation of the New Wilmington church and reconnecting with the friends she had made there while the boys were at college.

Finally, in 1945, the war ended. Pollock returned from Europe in one piece. He told his parents little about what he had seen there, but he did share his personal story of the horrible concentration camps the papers talked about. He was with the advanced forces of Seventh Army that liberated a group of prisoners . He said that as he walked through, seeing men who were just skin and bones, one man spoke to him. He saw the crosses on Pollock's lapels and said in German that he was a pastor too. Pollock carried that man out of the prison in his arms because he was too weak to walk. The pastor's name was Martin Niemöller; he was part of the Confessing Church in Germany that had opposed Hitler.

Early in 1946, Muriel and Pollock wrote that they were expecting a child in the summer. On the morning of July 29, Pollock called to tell them that they had another granddaughter, Elizabeth Paige. Both the baby and Muriel were expected to be fine, though it had been a difficult labor, and everyone was exhausted. Maud rushed to town to buy a pink woolen blanket to send the baby. When she got it home to wrap, Robert was pleased with her purchase and happy to see her so excited. Life in retirement was filled with an abundance of blessings for them, it seemed.

On August 1, Robert and Maud hosted a dinner party for friends, an early anniversary party and celebration of long friendships.

After the party, as they were going up to bed, Robert turned to Maud on the stairs and said, "We must do this more often."

He immediately collapsed, dead of a heart attack.

His life had been promised before his birth. He was born into a world of wagons and carts and horses and lamplight. He left the farm for university, never before having been away from upstate New York. He traveled to New Jersey and western Pennsylvania for his education. Rejection of his first application for mission service sent him to northern Michigan for a bitter-cold winter in a little church of people grateful to have him. The next year saw him off to the heat of India with his bride.

He had not done as much preaching and winning souls for Christ as he had done counting heads and finding land to buy and administering work in schools and hospitals. In that work, he had been a part of bringing education and medical care to generations of Indian people who had never had access to them before and of providing space for them to get to know people of faiths other than their own. He had lived to see electric lights replace lamps and automobiles take the place of bicycles and horses for transportation. He had lived through two wars and saw airplanes and bombs wreak far more distruction than troops on the ground could ever do. He had lost a daughter to death and been separated from a grandson, except for occasional pictures and notes to acknowledge gifts, by divorce. He wondered what it was that caused the two of his sons who had followed him into ministry to divorce the women they had sworn to love and live with til death parted them. He did not live to see Gandhi assisinated in 1948. He did not see Albert Einstein, humbled by the fact that the bomb he helped to create was used not against the Germans but against the Japanese, or Martin Neimöller, ashamed of himself and of his church for not speaking more strongly against the Nazis as they came to power, spend the rest of their lives working for global peace. Through all he had seen, he maintained unquenchable faith in the goodness of God, whose ways, though often unfathomable, are always just and good. And in the blink of an eye, it was over; his baptism was complete in death.

Maud called to Sharpe's, and the undertaker and coroner came at once to pronounce him dead and take his body to the funeral home.

As soon as he arrived at the funeral home, Mr. Sharpe called Pollock to let him know his father was dead. Pollock told Muriel, still in the hospital with the baby. Then he headed for New Wilmington, driving through the night. He arrived early in the morning and could not rouse his mother with his knocking.

He went to Sharpe's, where the undertaker welcomed him. To his question about his mother's unresponsiveness, Sharpe replied that she likely was sleeping soundly. They had all been up late. After coffee at the Sharpes and condolences from and catching up a little with the family, Pollock returned to his mother's house, where he found her in the kitchen. Over breakfast, he remarked that he was amazed at her calm. Maud smiled at her son and said that she knew she would grieve his father and miss him terribly.

Then she said, "But Pollock, how can I mourn today? This is the day he lived for, for seventy-five years. He has gone home to God."

REFERENCES

The Great Depression, 1930–1939. 2015. Americasbesthistory.com.

Anderson, Emma Dean, and Mary Jane Campbell. 1942. *In the Shadow of the Himalayas.* Philadelphia: Judson Press.

Andrews, Evan. March 12, 2015. "Remembering Gandhi's Salt March." History.com/news.

Annual Catalogue of the Allegheny Theological Seminary, 1896. Archive.org.archive.org/details/annualcatalogue189000alle.

Bostwick, Charles Byron. 1906. "Record of the Class of 1896 of Princeton University." Archive.org/details/record of class of 102prin.

Duryee, Ruth M. 1943. *Descendants of Robert McClellan Who Came to America in 1774.* Cambridge, New York.

Encyclopaedia Britannica. July 20, 2018. "Charles John Canning, Earl Canning." Britannica.com/biography/Charles-John-Canning-Earl-Canning.

Fahlbusch, Erwin. "Thomas the Apostle." Wikipedia.org/wiki/Thomas_the_Apostle#cite_note_Erwin_Fahlbusch.

History.com. 2010. "Stock Market Crash of 1929." History.com/topics/1929-stock-maraket-crash.

"Jack Hulme Directing Intra-Mural Athletics for Westminster Men." *New Castle News:* February 25, 1933.

Maxwell, Elizabeth. Family correspondence. Cambridge, New York: 1890–1925. Property of the Presbyterian Historical Society.

Maxwell, Robert. Correspondence with the Foreign Mission Office (UPNA). United Presbyterian Church. Robert Maxwell Correspondence, 1914–1942. Property of the Presbyterian Historical Society.

Niles, Damayanthi. 2012. *Worshipping at the Feet of Our Ancestors.* Zurich: Lit Verlag.

Niles, Daniel T. 1951. *That They May Have Life.* New York: Harper & Brothers.

Niles, D. Preman. 2004. *From East and West: Rethinking Christian Mission.* St. Louis: Chalice Press.

"Presbyterian Church (USA) Commission on Ecumenical Mission and Relations 1833–1966." 1966. Presbyterian Church (USA) Reports to General Assembly.

Smitha, Frank E. 200. "Macrohistory and World Timeline." www.fsmitha.com/time/ce19-9htm.

Staff, Woodstock School, "Woodstock School." Woodstockschool.in

"The Westminster Story." Westminster.edu.

Wikipedia. 2018. "Mahatma Gandhi." En.wikipedia.org.

Wikipedia. 2008. "Nankana massacre." En.wikipedia.org.

"World History Timeline 1901–1950." 2005. History-time line. depthi.com.

ACKNOWLEDGMENTS

Telling the story of a man I have always admired and never met has seemed a daunting task. Throughout the writing process, there were many without whom it would have been impossible. Among the Maxwells, there were my grandmother, Maud, my father, William Pollock, and his brother, Wallace, who told me stories about my grandfather. There was my great-aunt, Elizabeth, who saved letters home, and my cousin, Anne, who entrusted those letters to me. There were the people of the next generations, Phil and his son Luke, my nephews; Marianne, my niece; and my dear sons, Bill and Robert, who kept after me to tell the story. I will forever be indebted to Dr. Raj Nadella for his helping me to think about my grandfather's story as part of a much larger story of Christian mission on the subcontinent of India.

Many people I did not know helped more than I could have imagined, introducing me to other sources that offered a broader context of the time in which my grandfather lived and worked. There were the staff of the Presbyterian Historical Society in Philadelphia and the Pittsburgh Theological Seminary, who put in my hands documents I did not know existed: my grandfather's seminary catalogues and his correspondence with Dr. W. B. Anderson, secretary of the UPNA Foreign Mission Board. There was my grandfather's classmate at Princeton, C. B. Bostwick, class secretary, who compiled the ten-year reunion book, which tells much about life at Princeton in the four years the class of 1896 enjoyed and what became of them in the first decade after graduation. There were Emma Dean Anderson and Mary Jane Campbell, missionary friends of my grandparents, whose book, *In the Shadow of the Himalayas,* was published in 1942 and, thanks to Grandmother, made its way onto the bookshelves of her four sons. It is a precious treasure of the history of the Sialkot mission and gave me my first formal look at the work in which my grandparents took part. In their writing, three generations of the Niles family, Dr. D. T., Dr. Preman, and Dr. Damayanthi, taught me much about the church in South Asia, a community of believers established centuries before mission in the Western hemisphere, and the right relationships of partners in ministry together in God's world across cultures to each other and to the non-Christians they seek to serve. For historical background on the decades, I became hugely grateful for the ease of internet searches.

My writing partners in north Alabama, John Bush and Judy Rich, asked insightful questions that helped me clarify how I wanted to tell this story, not just about a man my family loved, but about mission work in the first half of the twentieth century through the lens of one family. Don Ruggles, grandson of William Merriam, shared with me his mother's memoir of her life in India, and we learned from the letters that our grandfathers shared a house for a while. Don read my manuscript and gave me his perspective, as another missionary grandkid with stories of his own, of the tale I was trying to tell. His sister-in-law, Patt Devitt, an inspiring devotional writer herself, taught me how to find a publisher. My high school classmate and friend, Nancy Owen Nelson, who now teaches writing, read the manuscript with her careful eye and gave me both encouragement and very helpful suggestions for clarification. The staff at West Bow Press have been unfailingly helpful throughout the publishing process. I am grateful for their patient shepherding of this first-time author. If this story makes sense, you can thank these folks, especially Nancy. If it bores you to tears, blame me. Retired preachers do tend to get caught up in their stories and ramble on.

ENDNOTES

1. Robert Maxwell. Family correspondence. Cambridge, New York: 1890–1925. March 13, 1890. Property of the Presbyterian Historical Society.
2. Ibid., March 7, 1890.
3. Ibid., March 15, 1890.
4. Ibid., March 7, 1890.
5. Ibid., May 19, 1900.
6. Ibid., June 12,1900.
7. Ibid., June 12, 1900.
8. Ibid., June 12, 1900.
9. Ibid., September 17, 1900.
10. Ibid., September 25, 1900.
11. "Presbyterian Church (USA) Commission on Ecumenical Mission and Relations 1833-1966." Presbyterian Church (USA) Reports to General Assembly, 1966.
12. Ibid.
13. Maxwell, 1890–1925. May 1, 1901.
14. Ibid., Feb. 1901
15. Ibid., Dec. 25, 1901.
16. Emma Dean Anderson and Mary Jane Campbell. *In the Shadow of the Himalayas.* Philadelphia: Judson Press, 1942, pp. 205-206.
17. Maxwell, 1890–1925. December 25, 1901.
18. Ibid., September 6, 1901.
19. Ibid.
20. Ibid.,1902, undated.
21. Ibid., March 12, 1902.
22. Ibid., June 23, 1902.
23. Ibid., June 2, 1902.
24. Ibid., October 13, 1902.
25. Ibid., April 1902
26. Ibid., undated.
27. Ibid., October 7, 1909.

[28] Robert Maxwell. Correspondence with the Foreign Mission Office (UPNA). United Presbyterian Church. Robert Maxwell Correspondence, 1914–1942. Property of the Presbyterian Historical Society.

[29] Ibid., received May 24, 1921.

[30] Ibid., January 6, 1925.

[31] Ibid., February 11, 1925.

[32] Ibid., February 17, 1931.

[33] Ibid., October 29, 1929.

[34] Ibid., May 19, 1930.

[35] Ibid., date unknown, 1935.

[36] Ibid., February 13, 1940.

[37] Ibid., April 15, 1941.

PHOTOGRAPHS

1. Robert and Charles Maxwell, p.13.
2. Robert and Maud Maxwell, p. 30.
3. George S. Maxwell with grandson, George Murdock, William Pollock, Robert Wallace and George Small Maxwell and Robert Murdock, p. 65.
4. The Maxwells 1918, p. 85.
5. Maud Maxwell, Maud's mother, Caroline Pollock, David and Wallace Maxwell, p. 104
6. R. J. and Elizabeth Maxwell, newlyweds, p. 112.
7. Robert Maxwell in retirement, p.135.

Printed in the United States
By Bookmasters